Witches' Spell-A-Day Almanac

Holidays & Lore
Spells, Rituals & Meditations

Copyright 2016 Llewellyn Worldwide Ltd.
Cover Design: Lisa Novak
Editing: Andrea Neff
Background photo: © PhotoDisc
Interior Art: © 2011, Steven McAfee
PP. 13, 33, 49, 71, 93, 113, 131, 151, 171, 191, 213, 231
Spell icons throughout: © 2011 Sherrie Thai

You can order Llewellyn books and annuals from *New Worlds*,
Llewellyn's catalog. To request a free copy of the catalog, call toll-free
1-877-NEW WRLD or visit our website at www.llewellyn.com.

ISBN: 978-0-7387-3768-3

Llewellyn is a registered trademark of Llewellyn Worldwide Ltd.
2143 Wooddale Drive
Woodbury, MN 55125

Printed in the United States of America

Contents

About the Authors

Barbara Ardinger, PhD (www.barbaraardinger.com), is the author of eight books, including *Secret Lives*, a novel about a circle of real-life women, plus goddesses, a talking cat, and the Green Man. Her day job is freelance editing for people who have good ideas but don't want to embarrass themselves in print. Barbara lives in Southern California with her two rescued Maine coon cats, Heisenberg and Schroedinger.

Elizabeth Barrette has been involved with the Pagan community for more than twenty-five years. She served as Managing Editor of *PanGaia* for eight years and Dean of Studies at the Grey School of Wizardry for four years. Her book *Composing Magic: How to Create Magical Spells, Rituals, Blessings, Chants, and Prayers* explains how to combine writing and spirituality. She lives in central Illinois, where she enjoys networking with local Pagans, such as coffeehouse meetings and open sabbats. Visit her blog, The Wordsmith's Forge (http://ysabetwordsmith.livejournal.com), or her website, PenUltimate Productions (http://penultimateproductions.weebly.com). Her coven site, with extensive Pagan materials, is Greenhaven Tradition (http://greenhaventradition.weebly.com).

Dallas Jennifer Cobb practices gratitude magic, giving thanks for personal happiness, health, and prosperity; meaningful, flexible, and rewarding work; and a deliciously joyful life. She is accomplishing her deepest desires. She lives in paradise with her daughter, in a waterfront village in rural Ontario, where she regularly swims and runs, chanting: "Thank you, thank you, thank you." Contact her at jennifer.cobb@live.com or visit www.magical living.ca.

Deborah Blake is the author of the Baba Yaga paranormal romance series, including *Wickedly Magical*, *Wickedly Dangerous*, *Wickedly Wonderful*, and *Wickedly Powerful* (Berkley) as well as nine books on modern Witchcraft from Llewellyn Worldwide. She has an ongoing column in *Witches & Pagans* magazine and was featured in *The Pagan Anthology of Short Fiction*. She can be found at www.deborahblakeauthor.com.

Emyme resides in New Jersey with her beloved cats, concentrating on candle and garden spells and kitchen witchery. In addition to writing poetry about strong women of mythology, she enjoys creating flash fiction with a modern twist on traditional fairy tales. A collection of her works is soon forthcoming. Emyme is looking forward to retirement and the opportunity

to devote more time to her writing and her craft—and the fresh challenge of being a grandmother. Please send questions or comments to catsmeow24 @verizon.net.

Boudica Foster is best known for her professional reviews of books on Paganism and its various paths. Boudica and her husband, Michael, ran the successful Wiccan/Pagan Times website and Facebook page. She also ran the Zodiac Bistro website, a repository of articles, commentaries, and reviews, for many years. Boudica is a staunch supporter of building Pagan community and has worked in covens as well as having a solitary practice. She has presented at many events in the Northeast and Ohio. She still presents occasionally at events and holds public workshops in the Northeast. She runs the website Boudica.net and reads tarot cards for clients. Boudica lives in Bucks County, PA, with her husband and cats.

Ember Grant has been writing for the Llewellyn annuals since 2003. She is the author of three books. Her latest is *The Second Book of Crystal Spells*. Visit her online at EmberGrant.com.

Devin Hunter is a professional Witch and medium who hails from San Francisco. He is a co-founder of Black Rose Witchcraft, author of *The Witch's Book of Power*, and the Witch King of the Sacred Fires Tradition of Witchcraft. His A.V. Club favorite podcast, *The Modern Witch*, has helped thousands of people develop their psychic and magical abilities. Visit him online for more information at DevinHunter.net.

James Kambos grew up in a family where folk magic was practiced. He's studied the folk magic traditions of Greece, the Near East, and the Appalachian region of the United States. He writes and paints from his home in Ohio.

Najah Lightfoot is a Priestess of the Goddess. She is a Witchvox Sponsor, a Lucky Mojo Certified Practitioner, and an active member of the Denver Pagan community. Najah is dedicated to keeping the Old Ways while living in these modern times. She enjoys movies, ritual, good food, and practicing the art of Shao-lin Kung Fu. Contact her at www.craftandconjure.com, www.facebook.com/priestessnajah, and www.twitter.com/priestess_najah.

Deborah Lipp is the author of seven books, including *Tarot Interactions: Become More Intuitive, Psychic & Skilled at Reading Cards* and *Merry Meet Again: Lessons, Life & Love on the Path of a Wiccan High Priestess*. Deborah has been Wiccan for most of her life and a High Priestess of the Gardnerian tradition for the past thirty years. She's been published in

newWitch, *Llewellyn's Magical Almanac*, *Pangaia*, and *Green Egg*. Deborah is also an avid media writer and blogger and is co-owner of Basket of Kisses: Smart Discussion About Smart Television (www.lippsisters.com). She lives in Jersey City with her spouse, Melissa, and an assortment of cats.

Estha McNevin (Missoula, MT) is a Priestess and ceremonial oracle of Opus Aima Obscuræ, a nonprofit Pagan temple haus. She has served the Pagan community since 2003 as an Eastern Hellenistic officiate, lecturer, freelance author, artist, and poet. Estha studies and teaches courses on ancient and modern Pagan history, multicultural metaphysical theory, ritual technique, international cuisine, organic gardening, herbal craft, alchemy, and occult symbolism. In addition to hosting public rituals for the sabbats, Estha organizes annual philanthropic fundraisers, Full Moon spellcrafting ceremonies, and women's divination rituals for each Dark Moon. To learn more, please explore www.facebook.com/opusaimaobscurae.

Gede Parma Akheron is a Wild Witch, Pagan mystic, initiated Priest, and award-winning author. He is an initiate and teacher of the WildWood Tradition of Witchcraft, a hereditary healer and seer with Balinese-Celtic ancestry, and an enthusiastic writer. Gede is a proactive and dynamic teacher and is also the creator and facilitator of the two-year Shamanic Craft Apprenticeship. He teaches both in Australia and internationally. Gede's spiritual path is highly syncretic, fusing a variety of Craft and mystic traditions. He is also the devoted priest and lover of Aphrodite, Hermes, Hekate, the Blue God, Persephone, and the Sacred Four of the WildWood.

Susan Pesznecker is a writer, college English teacher, nurse, practicing herbalist, and hearth Pagan/Druid living in northwestern Oregon. Sue holds a master's degree in professional writing and loves to read, watch the stars, camp with her wonder poodle, and work in her own biodynamic garden. She is co-founder of the Druid Grove of Two Coasts. Sue has authored *Yule*, *The Magickal Retreat*, and *Crafting Magick with Pen and Ink*. Visit her on her Web page (www.susanpesznecker.com) and Facebook author page (www.facebook.com/SusanMoonwriterPesznecker).

Laurel Reufner's mother can verify that she grew up a "wild child" in farming country. Laurel has been earth-centered for around a quarter century and really enjoys writing about whatever topics grab her attention. Laurel has always lived in southeastern Ohio and currently calls Athens County home, where she lives with her wonderful husband and two wild daughters of her own. Find her online at Laurel Reufner's Lair (laurelreufner.blogspot.com) or on Facebook.

A Note on Magic and Spells

The spells in the *Witches' Spell-A-Day Almanac* evoke everyday magic designed to improve our lives and homes. You needn't be an expert on magic to follow these simple rites and spells; as you will see if you use these spells throughout the year, magic, once mastered, is easy to perform. The only advanced technique required of you is the art of visualization.

Visualization is an act of controlled imagination. If you can call up in your mind a picture of your best friend's face or a flag flapping in the breeze, you can visualize. In magic, visualizations are used to direct and control magical energies. Basically the spellcaster creates a visual image of the spell's desired goal, whether it be perfect health, a safe house, or a protected pet.

Visualization is the basis of all good spells, and as such it is a tool that should be properly used. Visualization must be real in the mind of the spellcaster so it allows him or her to raise, concentrate, and send forth energy to accomplish the spell.

Perhaps when visualizing you'll find that you're doing everything right, but you don't feel anything. This is common, for we haven't been trained to acknowledge—let alone utilize—our magical abilities. Keep practicing, however, for your spells can "take" even if you're not the most experienced natural magician.

You will notice also that many spells in this collection have a some-what "light" tone. They are seemingly fun and frivolous, filled with rhyme and colloquial speech. This is not to diminish the seriousness of the purpose, but rather to create a relaxed atmosphere for the practitio-ner. Lightness of spirit helps focus energy; rhyme and common language help the spellcaster remember the words and train the mind where it is needed. The intent of this magic is indeed very serious at times, and magic is never to be trifled with.

Even when your spells are effective, magic won't usually sparkle before your very eyes. The test of magic's success is time, not immedi-ate eye-popping results. But you can feel magic's energy for yourself by rubbing your palms together briskly for ten seconds, then holding them a few inches apart. Sense the energy passing through them, the warm tin-gle in your palms. This is the power raised and used in magic. It comes from within and is perfectly natural.

Among the features of the *Witches' Spell-A-Day Almanac* are an easy-to-use "book of days" format; new spells specifically tailored for each day

of the year (and its particular magical, astrological, and historical energies); and additional tips and lore for various days throughout the year—including color correspondences based on planetary influences, obscure and forgotten holidays and festivals, and an incense of the day to help you waft magical energies from the ether into your space. Moon signs, phases, and voids are also included to help you find the perfect time for your rituals and spells.

Enjoy your days, and have a magical year!

Spell-A-Day Icons

New Moon

Full Moon

Abundance

Altar

 Balance

Clearing, Cleaning

Garden

Grab Bag

 Health, Healing

Home

 Heart, Love

Meditation, Divination

Money, Prosperity

 Protection

 Relationship

 Success

 Travel, Communication

Air Element

Earth Element

Fire Element

Spirit Element

 Water Element

Spells at a Glance by Date and Category*

	Health	Protection	Success	Heart, Love	Clearing, Cleaning	Home	Meditation, Divination
Jan.	5	7, 13, 30, 31	3, 26	16	18, 25	22	1, 11, 20, 23, 24, 29
Feb.	4, 5, 20, 22, 25, 27	7	6	21	8	15	2, 24
March	19		2, 7, 9, 30	11, 15	8, 19, 22, 25, 26, 29	3	1, 6
April	3		8, 9	7	12	16	4, 14, 30
May	4	2, 16, 28, 29	5, 9, 19, 20	13, 15	22	6	1, 21, 27, 31
June	1	17	7, 25		10, 14	2	6, 14, 16, 28
July	8, 20, 26, 28	29, 30	18, 25, 31	1	15	12, 24	13
Aug.	5, 24	11, 14, 22, 26	4, 23, 31	1, 25	10	3, 19	9, 16, 17, 20
Sept.	10	1, 19	15, 24, 28	21, 25	12, 27	22	7, 23, 30
Oct.	14, 21	2, 8, 10, 12, 22, 24, 27, 28	3, 17, 25	13		15, 20, 26	1
Nov.	13	6, 7, 10, 14, 27	28	26	2, 8, 9, 16	3, 19, 23	5
Dec.		5, 8	23, 31	19, 29	1, 11, 16, 22, 26, 28	15, 20, 25	30

*List is not comprehensive.

2017

Year of Spells

January

Before Julius Caesar hired the astronomer Sosigenes of Alexandria in 46 BCE to reform the calendar, the year began with the spring equinox. But the traditional calendar had gotten out of sync with the seasons. The new Julian calendar remained in effect until it, too, fell out of sync and was reformed in 1582 by Pope Gregory XIII. The Gregorian calendar is today's common calendar, though some religions still use variations of the Julian calendar.

January is named for Janus (Ianus), the two-faced Roman god of the doorway, which is the transition point between the safe indoors and the outside world, where anything might happen. Before Janus came to the city, he was Dianus, an Italian oak god whose consort was the woodland goddess Diana. The Romans weren't alone in believing that this opening needed to be protected. The mezuzah, which holds verses from Deuteronomy, is affixed to doors of Jewish houses. Medieval cathedrals feature elaborate façades around their doorways, and nearly every Pagan is taught to cut a "doorway" into the energy of the circle.

When we do January magic, let's focus on openings, closings, and transitions. What are we closing? What are we opening?

Barbara Ardinger, PhD

January 1

Sunday

1st ♒

Color of the day: Orange
Incense of the day: Almond

New Year's Day – Kwanzaa ends –
hanukkah ends

New Beginnings

Those New Year's resolutions you said you were not going to make but did? Here is a project to help you see them through to the end.

Keep them in a spell box. A spell box is a small, covered container made of whatever material you choose, designated to hold "spells in progress." The box can be a color that is appropriate to the kinds of spells you place in it. It reminds you to work on the spells in progress.

Place stones or herbs appropriate to the spells in the bottom of the box to give the spells energy. Write the intent of the spell and the chant that you devised on a piece of parchment. Tie each piece of parchment with raffia ribbon in a color that matches the spell intent, and keep the spells rolled up inside the box. Decorate the box with the appropriate stones or sigils. Pick out the spells and work on them regularly.

Boudica

January 2

Monday

1st ♒

☽ v/c 2:59 am

☽ → ♓ 4:57 am

Color of the day: Lavender
Incense of the day: Narcissus

Getting Divine help During a Mercury Retrograde

Several times a year, the planet Mercury seems to be moving backward in the sky. This is called Mercury retrograde. While other planets also move retrograde, Mercury seems to be the most troublesome. Things break down. People lose their tempers and make ridiculous mistakes. Murphy's law—"if anything can go wrong, it will"—takes over. When Mercury is retrograde, we are warned not to sign contracts and to think before we speak.

During a Mercury retrograde, speak to the god himself:

Great Mercury, even though you are walking backward right now, please remember that we mortals do better when going forward. Lend me your winged hat, which I will wear as a thinking cap that will straighten my thoughts and ideas and keep me from doing stupid things. Keep me safe until you go forward.

Or, more directly (so to speak):

Tricky planet, go direct right now!

Pesky Murphy, go away, don't bow!

Barbara Ardinger

NOTES:

January 3
Tuesday

1st ♓

Color of the day: White
Incense of the day: Ginger

Building Bridges

On January 3, 1870, construction began on the Brooklyn Bridge. Let's do a bridge-building spell.

Do you have a goal that seems impossible to reach? You need a bridge! For this spell, you will need some sculpting clay, a dish of water, and some embroidery thread.

Sculpt two "islands" of appropriate colors representing "today" and "goal." If your goal is wealth, then your goal island should be green. If you want romance, make it pink. Your thread should also be goal-colored.

Form a pillar on each island from which a bridge can be built.

Place the water dish between the finished islands. Speak the story of your problem: *I am _____ and I want _____, but I don't see a way to get it. I need a bridge.*

String the thread in a loop from the today island to the goal island and tie a knot. Say: *I am building a bridge.* Repeat nine times.

When you're ready, say three times: *I have a bridge! I will reach my goal!*

Deborah Lipp

January 4
Wednesday

1st ♓

☽ v/c 11:14 am

☽ → ♈ 11:20 am

Color of the day: Brown
Incense of the day: Lilac

World Braille Day

Today we celebrate Louis Braille for his genius invention of the Braille system of raised writing. His visionary creation brought reading, literature, and education to those with vision challenges. Just as it takes only one candle to illuminate the darkness, it took only one man to bring light to the masses.

For this spell, you will need twelve white candles, some Florida water, and a carving tool. Cleanse your candles with the Florida water. Carve any symbols or words that are special to you into the candles.

Close your eyes. Imagine what it would be like if you depended on your sensitive touch to read. Touch your candles, then open your eyes. Light one candle and take in its brilliant flame. Using this candle, light all the other candles. When finished, pinch out the candles while saying:

As above, so below. The magick is with me wherever I go.

Use the candles to light other candles throughout the year.

Najah Lightfoot

January 5
Thursday

1st ♈

2nd Quarter 2:47 pm

Color of the day: Purple
Incense of the day: Clove

An Ivy Spell

Traditionally this was the day ivy was used to divine what kind of health a person would experience during the coming year. Ivy was also used to protect the home from harmful energy during the winter months.

To predict your health for the rest of the year, you'll need an ivy leaf, a bowl of water, and a clean white cloth. First, place the ivy leaf in the bowl of water. Think of any health concerns you may have and cover the bowl with the cloth. Let it sit overnight undisturbed. Check the leaf the following morning. If the leaf has remained green and unblemished, you should have a healthy year. If the leaf has begun to darken or is covered with black spots, you should take steps to protect your health—get plenty of rest, watch your diet, and so on. To protect your home from negativity, keep an ivy plant near a window or door.

James Kambos

January 6
Friday

2nd ♈

☽ v/c 1:41 pm

☽ → ♉ 3:18 pm

Color of the day: Pink
Incense of the day: Rose

To honor Perchta

Today is the day of Frau Perchta, a Norse goddess associated with the wilderness, spinning, and even the Wild Hunt in some parts of Germany. On this night, folks would leave offerings of food out for her, hoping for her blessings of good luck in the coming year. Why not honor Perchta by leaving some cream and a hearty slice of bread out for her? And ask her for blessings throughout the year by creating some sort of simple weaving project, perhaps for use on your altar. Those simple weaving looms that use loops of fabric are very easy to work with and make great coasters and hot pads. Similar looms can also easily be made using cardboard. Check around the Web.

Laurel Reufner

January 7
Saturday

2nd ♉

☽ v/c 9:23 pm

Color of the day: Indigo
Incense of the day: Sage

Spell for Things That Go Bump in the Night

We're still in the year's darkest months, and the night can be full of bumps and chills. Protect yourself from disturbances with a charm for peaceful sleep.

Make a simple drawstring bag by sewing a large running stitch around the edges of a five- or six-inch circle of fabric and gathering it into a pouch.

Fill the pouch with a piece of snowflake obsidian (for grounding and protection), a pinch each of mugwort (for dreams) and sage (for peaceful sleep), a few rose petals (for comfort and emotional security), some lavender (relaxation), and a small feather. On a small piece of paper, write BUMP and draw a line through it. Add this to the bag, too.

Tie the bag shut with a piece of string, fastening it with a square knot to invoke elemental protection. Leave the string ends long to trap negative energies. Hang the bag from your headboard or nightstand. Sweet dreams be yours!

Susan Pesznecker

January 8
Sunday

2nd ♉

☽ → ♊ 5:06 pm

Color of the day: Amber
Incense of the day: Eucalyptus

Casting Eternal Light

Cleanse a Swarovski aquamarine baroque-style drop pendant with saltwater. This starry gemstone is evocative of January's blue-hued dawn light, an iconic time of solar regeneration. From 5:00 a.m. until 1:00 p.m. today, hang the pendant in a mistletoe or willow tree. If you cannot access such a tree, find a nearby balcony railing, fence line, or shrub, and tie on a spring of willow or mistletoe, imbibing this solar tree energy.

Suspend the crystal so it hangs freely and will receive direct sunlight throughout the morning. When the first solar glow refracts into rainbows, chant this Kabalistic affirmation:

Nimble creation and earthly formation, reside and radiate your perpetually vivid light. O Solar Yod (light), a spark spun of Ain Sof (eternity), nurture your bright fountain of splendor within this gem.

Wear this crystal for healing work or ceremony, or gift as needed. Store your pendant in golden felt and repeat this affirmation to recharge it any time.

Estha McNevin

January 9
Monday

2nd ♊

Color of the day: Gray
Incense of the day: Hyssop

Winds of Renewal

Start your day with a refreshing blast of winter air. Focus on renewal, even though it may appear bleak outside. The air element brings change and opportunity. Visualize any specific opportunity or change you're hoping for, or just remain open to whatever comes your way. Try to actually feel the air on your face several times today. Whisper these words to the wind:

Winter wind, what secrets you must keep, blowing in the night, howling while we sleep.

Winter wind, what promises you make, stirring morning snow as you whisper us awake.

Though you may be harsh and cold, on your breath rewards untold.

Repeat throughout the day, if desired, or again at night before bedtime.

Ember Grant

January 10
Tuesday

2nd ♊

☽ v/c 4:38 pm

☽ → ♋ 5:49 pm

Color of the day: Black
Incense of the day: Bayberry

happy and Prosperous

Invoke Ebisu, the jolly Japanese god of commerce. Plan for a financially sound year by setting a simple budget. Make a spreadsheet (using Excel or OpenOffice) to track the coming twelve months. Under "Expenses," list all of your regular expenses, including utilities, housing, food, insurance, transportation, medical, dental, entertainment, and recreation. Under "Income," list all sources of money that flow to you, such as wages, trust funds, child support, disability allowance, and government support payments.

Knowledge is power, and knowing exactly what you earn and spend will give you the power to manage your finances wisely. Place the budget on your altar with a coin, an offering to Ebisu, and say:

Bless me, Ebisu, you happy, prosperous god. May I have sufficient resources to cover my expenses. May I be happy. May I earn more than I spend.

Review your budget monthly, adding current data.

Dallas Jennifer Cobb

January 11
Wednesday

2nd ♋

Color of the day: Yellow
Incense of the day: Lavender

Carmenta Spell for Prophecy

Today is the first of two feast days for the Roman goddess Carmenta, who is known for her gifts of retrocognition and prophecy. On this sacred day known as Carmentalia, she is invoked by her two epithets, Postvorta and Antevorta. She is given offerings of rice or grain and incense smoke, and is asked to guide us as we look into both the past and the future.

This spell is cast to aid in divination and should be done at dusk or dawn for best results. In a large coffee mug filled with hot water, steep five bay leaves, one cinnamon stick, and half of a small, fresh orange (squeeze the juice over the cinnamon stick, then place the entire half in the mug). Add one tablespoon honey, and as you stir, say the following incantation:

Carmenta Postvorta, Carmenta Antevorta,

She of dream and of hill, awaken now a heightened skill!

Prophecy rising, soul set free, as I drink I summon thee!

Devin hunter

January 12
Thursday

2nd ♋

☽ v/c 6:34 am

Full Moon 6:34 am

☽ → ♌ 7:08 pm

Color of the day: Crimson

Incense of the day: Jasmine

Moon Magic for a New Year

This is the first full moon of the new year, which makes it the perfect time to get your intentions for the coming year off to a good start. Take a few moments to figure out what your goals and intentions are, then write them down on a piece of paper. Light a white candle and say the following, holding those intentions in your heart:

Blessed moon on a new year shine,

Illuminate these goals of mine.

Make me worthy, make me strong,

And guide my path all year long.

Deborah Blake

January 13
Friday

3rd ♌

Color of the day: Rose

Incense of the day: Thyme

Lemon, Clove, and Salt Spell

Every now and then we may feel the need to reinforce our wards, our boundaries, our shields. This spell draws upon Italian folk magic and three simple ingredients found in many homes: lemon, clove, and salt.

Ground, center, and align. Go to the kitchen or a working space that is embedded in your day-to-day home life. Take the bright yellow lemon, which has solar associations, and begin to draw up empowered breath from the earth and the worlds below. Breathe seven times over the lemon and perceive it glowing; perhaps you even hear a buzzing. Push thirteen cloves into the lemon, each time focusing on reinforcing the wards of yourself and your home. Finally, lay the lemon-and-cloves spell in a bowl containing rock salt, and do so with purpose and power. So mote it be.

Gede Parma

January 14

Saturday

3rd ♌

☽ v/c 10:17 am

☽ → ♍ 10:52 pm

Color of the day: Brown
Incense of the day: Pine

Go Fly a Kite

Today is International Kite Day. Gather your family or coven for an entertaining day of kite creation.

Kites may be elaborate or simple, able to fly or merely decorative. Many books and websites are devoted to kite construction. Store-bought kites can be personalized. Write blessings and requests on the kite or on the tail section(s). If you are aiming for a functional type of kite or going with a pre-made kite, leave enough room at the end of the day for flying, weather permitting. Or you may simply enjoy the day creating a kite to be used in the future.

Call upon the air element, the wind gods and goddesses, and air spirits to assist in your creation and flight. Bless and cleanse your kite with a sage stick, and repeat the following or create your own spell:

Keepers of the wind, we ask you to blow gently and carry this kite aloft.

Let it play in the sky and dance among the sylphs.

However it please you, bring it safely back to earth.

Or let it go to find another partner and rise again some other day.

Emyme

NOTES:

January 15
Sunday

3rd ♍

Color of the day: Gold
Incense of the day: Juniper

Light Away the Blues

Cold days and long, dark nights are challenging for the best of us, but even more so for those affected by seasonal affective disorder (SAD). Our ability to light our way in the darkness has always been one of our most important needs.

For this spell, gather one candle for each of the four directions and one white candle for spirit. You will also need one small sage bundle.

Light the white candle and then use it to light the other four candles.

Light your smudge stick. Pass the smoke over your lighted candles while saying:

Spirit, blessed, powerful, and bright,

I am always surrounded by the light.

Darkness has no place in me,

For by your light, I see clearly.

Repeat this ritual whenever you need a lift from the dark days of winter or anytime you are feeling blue.

Najah Lightfoot

January 16
Monday

3rd ♍

Color of the day: Silver
Incense of the day: Lily

Birthday of Martin Luther King Jr.

Peace Be with You

Words carry power. And when words are used intentionally as invocations, the power is magnified.

An invocation is a means of asking for assistance, figuratively "invoking" power from another source. Today we celebrate Martin Luther King Jr.'s birthday. King spent his life working to bring peace to the world and all its people, and today you can continue his work by invoking his assistance, using his words of power, and speaking his wishes aloud.

Each time you meet someone today—whether in person, by phone, or online—begin your conversation with "peace be with you." You'll be calling upon King to stand with you. As you do so, your words will become magick, filled with intention as you offer each person a blessing of peace. For added oomph, wear white today and light white candles on your altar. Peace be with you!

Susan Pesznecker

January 17
Tuesday

3rd ♍

☽ v/c 1:09 am

☽ → ♎ 6:16 am

Color of the day: Maroon
Incense of the day: Cinnamon

Blessing Our Electronic Devices

Yes, of course we stand before our altars and invoke and work with the pantheons of classical Greece or Rome, India, or Northern Europe. But where do we do our real day-to-day work? On our devices. Who has a landline these days? How often do we sit down at our desktop computers? Who these days knows what a typewriter is? Who sends anything via snail mail?

But, alas, our devices occasionally fail us. Just like us, they need regular "meals"; that is, they need to be regularly recharged. Here's an invocation to draw down and pull in the power:

Chargers, chargers, in your sockets,

Make my 'tronics run like rockets.

PC, laptop, smartphone, tablet,

Power every app and applet.

Barbara Ardinger

January 18
Wednesday

3rd ♎

Color of the day: White
Incense of the day: Honeysuckle

Break a Bad Habit Song

We all have those bad habits we wish we could stop. But we need to want to change for it to happen. Spells are all about change. Biting our nails and not picking up after ourselves are simple habits we can break ourselves.

Breaking a habit starts with you wanting to break it. Then it takes time to work the habit into something positive. Repetition is the way to create a good habit out of the old. Spell chants remind you to create this new pattern of behavior. You use a familiar piece of music and just rewrite the words. Make it an earworm that will pop into your head in times of stress. Write a short chant to help you remember your focus and objective. Sing it, even if it is just in your head. Use as needed.

Boudica

January 19
Thursday

3rd ♎

☽ v/c 3:55 am

☉ → ≈ 4:24 pm

☽ → ♏ 5:09 pm

4th Quarter 5:13 pm

Color of the day: Turquoise
Incense of the day: Myrrh

Invocations to Oyuki

Oyuki, or Yuki-onna, is a Japanese snow spirit. She can be perilous in person, appearing as a pale woman with long black hair who can freeze unwary travelers in their tracks. But she can also be asked to bring or to banish snowstorms. Here is an incantation for each purpose.

To attract snow:

Oyuki, spirit
of the winter snow and wind,
come and dance for me

bring long hair blowing
and white kimono swirling
and cold wet kisses

come forth, Oyuki,
and let us dance together
in this frozen time

To repel snow:

Oyuki, goddess
of blizzards and wintertime,
pass by this place now

lift up your white robes
and tie back your wild hair
and close your cold lips

go on, Oyuki;
some other time we shall play
but not here, not now
                    Elizabeth Barrette

NOTES:

January 20
Friday

4th ♏

Color of the day: Coral
Incense of the day: Vanilla

Inauguration Day

Beauty Affirmation

Since the moon is waning now, use this time to focus inward, contemplating and meditating. Consider beauty. It is not merely physical, and it's certainly in the eyes of the beholder. But don't forget how much of beauty is actually your attitude and behavior—your spirit and actions.

Do something today that makes you feel good. Donate to charity, spend time with loved ones, or pamper yourself. Meditate on how beautiful you are, child of the stars. And tell others how beautiful they are as well. Whenever you feel uncertain of your true beauty, recall these words:

I am body, mind, and soul,

A unique and perfect whole.

Beautiful inside and out,

Remember this and never doubt.

Ember Grant

January 21
Saturday

4th ♏

☽ v/c 8:24 pm

Color of the day: Blue
Incense of the day: Ivy

Like a Virgin

Today the Romans traditionally honored Saint Agnes, patron saint of chastity, so it seems like a great time to think "like a virgin." But wait, let's go back to the original meaning of the word. A virgin was a woman not under the care and control of a father, brother, or husband; an autonomous woman, independent and not required to answer to any man or child. According to Marilyn Frye, author of *Willful Virgin*, "virgins are wild and willful humans, not subjugated property."

Today, regardless of your gender, act like a virgin. Close your eyes and picture yourself as a wild and willful human. How do you dress? What do you desire? Who do you love? How do you live your life? Now open your eyes and spend the day living like a virgin. You may choose to hold on to your virginity for a long, long time.

Dallas Jennifer Cobb

January 22

Sunday

4th ♏

☽ → ♐ 5:45 am

Color of the day: Yellow
Incense of the day: Marigold

hearth and home happiness

The dark, cold months of winter are a good time to hunker down and stay close to home. But that doesn't mean you can't have fun or enjoy a little indulgence to get you through the season. If you are someone who struggles with the lack of light (or even if you're not), try this spell to bring a little more enjoyment into your time at home. Be sure to finish up with something special, whether that is a nice piece of chocolate or a hot bath with a good book (or all three!). Say:

I call in joy and I call in light

To bring some warmth on a winter's night.

Fun, indulgence, friends, and cheer,

I welcome all to my home so dear.

Deborah Blake

January 23

Monday

4th ♐

Color of the day: Ivory
Incense of the day: Clary sage

A Garnet Meditation

Garnet, the birthstone for January, is also a great all-purpose gem to use as an aid during meditation. It can be used to help make decisions or bring order to your life.

For this meditation, you'll need a garnet gem or a smooth garnet stone. A string of garnet prayer beads would also work. Select a deep red garnet or one with a brown tint. You'll also need a burgundy candle. Begin by lighting the candle, then relax and center. Hold the garnet and breathe deeply. Concentrate on your concern and then hold the garnet to your heart. You'll begin to receive messages. Let them come, even if they don't make sense. When you feel ready to return to your everyday world, extinguish the candle. Thank the garnet for its help. Your thoughts should be clearer now so you can make any decision.

James Kambos

January 24
Tuesday

4ħ ♐

☽ v/c 12:33 pm

☽ → ♑ 5:43 pm

Color of the day: Gray
Incense of the day: Geranium

One Step at a Time

John Belushi was born on January 24, 1949. A gifted comedian, he died at age thirty-three of a drug overdose.

Meditate today on releasing yourself from addictions that prevent you from using your natural-born gifts.

Addiction may not be drugs or alcohol for you. It's whatever or whoever you're so attached to that it could ruin your life.

Today's meditation is just one step on a journey away from addiction. Begin by acknowledging that. Maybe it's your first step, maybe it's your hundredth. Bless and embrace your step, whatever step it is.

As you meditate on letting go, don't forget what you keep. Like Belushi, you have a gift—the love in your heart, an art, a talent—something uniquely your own. Remember that every step away from addiction is a step toward fully realizing that gift.

Meditate on addiction falling away from you, and visualize the beauty and talent that remain.

Deborah Lipp

NOTES:

January 25
Wednesday

4th ♑

Color of the day: Topaz
Incense of the day: Bay laurel

A Room of One's Own

There's no need to tell you how important it is to have a sacred space, a sanctuary. Make this the day you cleanse that room and perform a winter cleaning.

If possible, remove everything from the room and clean it with all-natural cleansers from ceiling to floor. Cleanse every item you return to the room, and replace anything worn or unused.

Or take this day to find and create a room in which to practice your craft. Should you be lucky enough to have options, ask your deity of choice to help you in choosing a room. A south-facing room is best, but work with what you have. Go all out and empty the room and then cleanse, paint, and refloor it, or merely cleanse it in whatever fashion you choose. Create an altar, and bring in a cabinet or chest of drawers for your supplies.

When you are done, relax, content with your work, in a room of your own. Say:

Bless my work is all I ask.

Ere I begin this sacred task.

A strong back, no idle hand,

Create with me a soft place to land.

Emyme

NOTES:

January 26
Thursday

4th ♑

Color of the day: Green
Incense of the day: Nutmeg

Midnight Oil

Some people do their best work at night. Others don't, but need to work at night anyway. Here is a spell for enhancing your accomplishments after dark. It gathers ambient energy from the sun and moon to aid you.

For this spell, you will need an oil lamp and some oil. The lamp doesn't need to be big—you can use the candle-sized kind if you wish.

First set the oil in a sunny place from dawn to dusk. Say over it:

Hour by hour,

Drink the sun's power.

Then set the oil where it will be bathed by moonlight from dusk to dawn. Say over it:

Hour by hour,

Drink the moon's power.

Once the oil has been charged, fill the lamp with it. Whenever you're working at night and need a boost, light the oil lamp and say:

Now the time is right;

Give to me the light.

Elizabeth Barrette

January 27
Friday

4th ♑

☽ v/c 2:18 am
☽ → ♒ 3:37 am
New Moon 7:07 pm

Color of the day: Purple
Incense of the day: Violet

Melodious Love Chimes

Today is the anniversary of Mozart's birth. Why not celebrate while strengthening a love affair at the same time? Buy a set of wind chimes with a melodious tone to hang in your home. You will also need some jasmine oil. Place the chimes in your home where the two of you spend the most time. Holding the bottle of oil in your hands, charge it with the love that the two of you have for each other and then anoint the chimes every month or so to keep that energy fresh. At least once a day, stop and bump the chimes to make them "sing."

Laurel Reufner

January 28
Saturday

1st ♒

Color of the day: Black
Incense of the day: Patchouli

Chinese New Year (Rooster)

happiness and Prosperity

Today marks the start of the year of the Rooster. Before alarm clocks, the rooster's crow woke people in time for work. The rooster is associated with punctuality and attention and wards off evil spirits.

Traditional Chinese New Year greetings include the Cantonese phrase *Kung hei fat choi*, which translates to "happiness and prosperity." The color red wards off bad luck and misfortune, and many Chinese wear red underwear at the New Year and hang red lanterns in their home.

Use red paper to make an offering envelope, carefully folding and gluing it. If you live in an urban area, you'll find red envelopes in most dollar stores. Because 5, 7, and 8 are lucky numbers for Rooster, enclose $5, $7, or $8 in the envelope and give it to a child or senior, bestowing a blessing on them. It's believed that how you act today influences your luck for the year. Be generous and happy. Know prosperity.

Dallas Jennifer Cobb

January 29
Sunday

1st ♒

☽ v/c 12:52 am
☽ → ♓ 11:10 am

Color of the day: Orange
Incense of the day: Frankincense

Candle and Well Spell

In the Northern Hemisphere, the seasonal powers are about to move through the door of the quickening, also known as Imbolc, Brighid, and Candlemas. Even if you are not in the Northern Hemisphere, this spell will work at any time of the year, or you could wait for August in the Southern Hemisphere.

Take a white candle and a dark ceramic bowl. Ground, center, and align yourself. Drop more deeply into your breath and begin to rock or sway back and forth or side to side. Feel the rhythm of the power that begins to move. It is almost like a serpent. Light the candle and gaze down into the bowl (the well) when you feel entranced and chant:

Candle and well,

This holy spell.

Open the gate,

For my vision awakes.

Open to perceive with your intuition. When you are finished, ground and eat something salty and dark.

Gede Parma

January 30
Monday

1st ♓

Color of the day: White
Incense of the day: Neroli

Dreamtime Courage

Here is a spell to thwart the shadows of the dream world. Just before bed, gather three glasses of water, three pennies, and three sugar cubes. Place the glasses in a row under the center of your bed, then drop in the pennies and finally add in the sugar cubes. Crawl into bed, and as you drift off to sleep, recite the following rhyme:

Pennies three, sweetened for me, cast a refractive security.

If the spell was successful, a series of safe dreams will prove the affirmation. The glasses will keep for up to three nights and provide the astral body with a shield for the dream world. To help redirect the flow of your body energy as you sleep, true copper pennies minted before 1982 will work best. Avoid our modern copper-plated zinc imposters, as, sadly, not all pennies are lucky these days.

Estha McNevin

January 31
Tuesday

1st ♓

☽ v/c 12:36 pm
☽ → ♈ 4:46 pm

Color of the day: Scarlet
Incense of the day: Ylang-ylang

Theft Protection Spell

Without a doubt, you have given or gotten some fancy new things over the holidays and might be concerned about them taking a walk on their own when you aren't looking. Let's face it: if something were to happen to that new phone or MP3 player, your heart would be crushed!

To protect an item from theft, burn equal parts clove, patchouli, and peppermint leaf over a charcoal in a fire-safe dish, and either pass the item through the aromatic smoke or gently fan the smoke over the item. While doing so, say the following spell:

Wall of thunder, cracked like a whip, protect my things from taking a trip!

Unless I will it, they be mine, guard them from thieves both mundane and divine.

Wall of protection, I summon you high, by clove and smoke no thief will try!

This is my will, and so shall it be, for the good of all but mostly for me!

Devin Hunter

February

February is the second and shortest month of the year. Named after the Latin word *februum*, it means "purification." This corresponds with the purification ritual of Februa on the full moon, originally the 15th in the ancient Roman calendar. Do some late-winter or early-spring cleaning. Get the whole coven involved in cleaning the covenstead.

Foreign names reveal more. In Old English, February was called Solmonath, which means "mud month," or Kale-monath, which refers to cabbage. The Slovene name Sveçan invokes Candlemas. The Finnish name Helmikuu means "month of the pearl," in which melting snow forms pearly drops of ice on the trees. In Polish this is Luty, the "month of ice," and in Czech it's Únor, when the river ice submerges. Native American names include Wolf Moon, Snow Moon, and Wind Moon.

This month is said to foreshadow the weather in the warm season. A wet February suggests a pleasant and fruitful summer. A dry, clear month hints at trouble to come. You can see echoes of this in Groundhog Day, where again foul weather predicts fair.

February honors Aradia, Brigid, and Juno Februa. It also features the Maiden Goddess and the consort God as Youth or Rogue.

Elizabeth Barrette

February 1
Wednesday

1st ♈

Color of the day: Brown
Incense of the day: Marjoram

An Abundance Spell

In the Eastern Orthodox Church, today is the feast day of St. Tryphon (Trypho). He's the protector of gardeners, fields, and vineyards. St. Tryphon not only protects gardens and crops but is also prayed to for growth and abundance. This celebration is linked to the ancient Greek god Dionysus, god of wine and fertility.

To help bring abundance into your life, rise just before dawn, face east, and say three things that you're grateful for. Then state three wishes you want to come true. Later sometime this evening, drape your altar with a green cloth and upon it place a glass of red wine and a new houseplant. Thank the Divine Power for all that you have and drink the wine. Tend the houseplant with great care and watch your abundance grow.

James Kambos

February 2
Thursday

1st ♈

☽ v/c 11:50 am
☽ → ♉ 8:50 pm

Color of the day: Crimson
Incense of the day: Carnation

Imbolc ~ Groundhog Day

Into the Light

At Imbolc, we are "in the belly" of the mother, and like little seeds under the soil, we are quickening with ideas and inspiration. Halfway between solstice and equinox, it's a good time to invoke faith, hope, and sunshine using a creativity spell. You'll need a couple magazines, scissors, a glue stick, a paper to stick stuff on, and your imagination. Close your eyes and envision the sun, glorious, bright, and radiant. Let your faith conjure up radiance. Feel hope grow. Now open your eyes and get to work, pulling images and words from the magazines that resonate with your vision. Trim them and create a collage honoring Brighid. Place it on your altar and light a candle. Say:

Brighid, bless these simple seeds, planted deep inside of me.

Let them sprout with growing light and grow my future safe and bright.

So mote it be.

Dallas Jennifer Cobb

February 3

Friday

1st ♉

2nd Quarter 11:19 pm

Color of the day: Rose
Incense of the day: Orchid

Warm heart

It's easy to become crabby with people if you are stuck in the house together. In truth, relationships can be tough no matter what the season. This is a simple spell to help you remember to be kind and patient, both with others and with yourself. If you want, you can light a red or pink candle while you say this spell:

Goddess, fill me with kindness.

Help me to be patient and loving

And to remember always

To keep your warmth of spirit in my heart

And to share it with others.

Deborah Blake

February 4

Saturday

2nd ♉

☽ v/c 5:42 pm

☽ → ♊ 11:44 pm

Color of the day: Gray
Incense of the day: Magnolia

Start Your Day the healthy Way

Some of us manage to stay healthy by eating our veggies. The rest of us would like to eat better. Really, we would! But with our busy schedules, it's hard to do more than invade the lunchroom at work (donuts, bagels, yummy!) and grab a fast-food lunch. And supper? In the car or in front of the TV, do we ever pay attention to what we're putting in our bodies?

Like Mother always said, "Take your vitamins." Here's an invocation to utter as you're swallowing that handful of health-giving supplements:

Jolly vitamins A, B, C,

Helpful D and all the rest,

Probiotics, min'rals, supplements,

Let's start my day the healthiest.

Daily multi, you go down with Coke or water

Or something just a little stronger.

No more cold pizza, nothing fraughter.

Help me live happier and longer!

Barbara Ardinger

February 5
Sunday

2nd ♊

Color of the day: Yellow
Incense of the day: Heliotrope

Long Life

Here is a spell to promote longevity and ward off illness.

Use a stone associated with longevity, such as agate, jade, a fossil, or petrified wood.

Dip the stone into saltwater, saying:

> I consecrate this stone of long life by water and earth. Long life, fill this sacred stone!

Pass the stone through sage smoke, saying:

> I consecrate this stone of long life by fire and air. Long life, fill this sacred stone!

Touch the stone to the top of your head, saying:

> Long life, fill my head!

Then touch and fill your heart, hands, and feet.

Now place the stone anywhere on your body that disease runs in your family—for example, the breasts for breast cancer—saying:

> Sacred stone, protect me and keep me well.

Do as many areas of the body as necessary.

Keep the stone on your altar. You can renew this spell periodically, always during a full or waxing moon.

Deborah Lipp

Notes:

February 6
Monday

2nd ♊

☽ v/c 5:53 pm

Color of the day: Silver
Incense of the day: Rosemary

Spell for Courage and Pluck

Most of us can use a little boost of courage and support from time to time. Creating a courage talisman may be just the thing.

Work in the period leading up to a full moon. Begin by cutting two two-inch squares from a piece of red felt. Sew the squares together on three sides, then add the following: a pinch of dragon's blood incense (for power), a small piece of labradorite (mental clarity), a small piece of blue ribbon (a prize!), and nine whole cloves (awareness and insight). For extra oomph, prick your finger and add a dab of your blood to the mixture. Sew the bag closed.

Consecrate and dedicate the talisman at high noon. Holding it in both hands, raise it to the sky and say:

Talisman of pluck, I offer thee,

And ask that you give nerve to me.

Keep the talisman on your person, reflecting on it often.

Susan Pesznecker

 February 7
Tuesday

2nd ♊

☽ → ♋ 2:03 am

Color of the day: Red
Incense of the day: Cedar

The North Wind Blows

Winter brings icy air, chilly nights, and tales of the bone-chilling power of the north wind. In some parts of the country, the winter wind is called the *hawk*, and you definitely don't want to be caught outside when the hawk is flying.

North is the direction of wisdom. In the face of adversity, we can hold on to wisdom, which sustains and grounds us. We can wrap ourselves in love and protection and face the winds of life, secure in the knowledge that we are always loved, guided, and protected.

Bundle yourself up, go outside, and invoke the power of the north wind. If you live in the Southern Hemisphere, you can use a fan to simulate a cold wind blowing.

Say:

Though the winds of change blow,

I am protected wherever I go.

In adversity and strife,

I am in charge of my life.

Najah Lightfoot

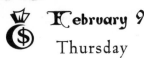

 # February 8
Wednesday

2nd ♋

☽ v/c 5:00 pm

Color of the day: Topaz
Incense of the day: Lavender

Clearing School Obstacles

Need to get back to school? Need some help overcoming obstacles in doing so? Try this spell for some added help.

In the middle of a heavy piece of paper, write what it is you want to accomplish educationally and circle it. Next, in the outside edges, write all of the things that are holding you back, such as money or time. Using a different colored ink, cross out those things one by one.

Now place a yellow candle in the middle of the paper and ring it with four green candles. Tonight, allow the green candles to burn down about an inch or so. Starting tomorrow, light all of the candles and allow them to burn for thirty minutes. Continue each night until they are gone. Now go out there and get to work. Put those helpful energies to use!

Laurel Reufner

February 9
Thursday

2nd ♋

☽ → ♌ 4:41 am

Color of the day: Green
Incense of the day: Balsam

Prosperity Spell

Often we work with the element of earth for prosperity, but today, since the moon is in Leo, we'll use the fire element. Choose some stones associated with both the element of fire and prosperity—stones such as pyrite and tiger's eye. You can also use jewelry such as gold chains or bracelets, especially ones set with diamonds.

Gather as many stones and pieces of jewelry as you can and arrange them around the outside of a green candle in a heatproof container. Visualize the abundance you need—extra money to pay bills, perhaps, or a raise at work. See yourself comfortable. Light the candle and chant:

By the stones and by the flame,

Prosperity is mine to claim.

Allow the candle to burn out completely. Keep the stones on your altar for as long as you like. If you used jewelry, wear it.

Ember Grant

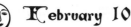 **February 10**

Friday

2nd ♌

Full Moon 7:33 pm

Color of the day: Purple
Incense of the day: Rose

Lunar Eclipse

A Full Moon Meditation

This full moon is accompanied by a lunar eclipse. An event such as this will create a great deal of energy in the environment around us, as well as inside us. This is a perfect time for meditation, problem-solving, and chanting. I would avoid casting any spells not just today but for two days before and after this eclipse as well.

Instead of doing spellwork, try this meditation. At the time of the eclipse, cover your altar with a gray cloth. Place three candles upon the altar in this order: one white, one black, and one white candle. Think of an issue in your life and light the first white candle. Next light the black candle and think of ways your issue might be solved. Lastly, light the second white candle. Does any particular way to solve your problem stand out in your mind now? If so, then there's your answer.

James Kambos

February 11

Saturday

3rd ♌

☽ v/c 12:52 am

☽ → ♍ 8:52 am

Color of the day: Blue
Incense of the day: Pine

Ancestral Ceremony

In the early morning, sit at your ancestral altar or before your family mantel. Concentrate on the photos of your family; focus on those who have crossed over. When you are ready to begin, clap your hands once to summon all of your genetic ancestors. While they are visiting, burn sandalwood or frankincense incense to bless them. Talk openly and freely about your hopes, dreams, fears, or troubles.

Speak fondly of any ancestors you have memories of. Think back to the times you shared. Finally, burn ancestral money paper—blank checks and copied bank statements—to transmute earthly wealth into spiritual currency for your ancestors to use in the afterlife. Clap your hands to end the ceremony.

For further luck, bless a bowl of fresh fruit with the incense smoke and then share the fruit with family and friends throughout the day.

Estha McNevin

February 12

Sunday

3rd ♍

Color of the day: Gold
Incense of the day: Juniper

Peppermint Spell

Take a bright green candle and some peppermint essential oil. Ground, center, and align. Anoint the candle with the oil from top to center and then from base to center; this is drawing in and attracting prosperity. Focus your entire mindfulness on this action. Know that you are charging the candle with your strength of intention.

When you are ready, begin to dance and clap and drum or rattle. Raise the power from the earth and call it down from the stars. Feel how it fills your whole self. You may feel like chanting:

Peppermint and candle green,

I call to make seen from unseen.

Prosperity mine,

By the power of nine!

Chant these words a minimum of nine times. Then, to release the power into the charged candle, clap nine times and throw the power into the wick. Light it and the spell is released.

Gede Parma

February 13

Monday

3rd ♍

☽ v/c 7:36 am

☽ → ♎ 3:43 pm

Color of the day: Lavender
Incense of the day: Clary sage

Wonderful You

We don't always see ourselves as we really are. We tend to be critical of ourselves. Here is a way to soften the rough edges. Let's make time for ourselves.

Start with a shower or bath. Good smells are essential. Use favorite soaps and shampoos that contain calming fragrances like lavender or rose. Add mint or lemon to bring a refreshing feel to the experience. Smells that are familiar bring about relaxation and calmness. Focus on acceptance of who you are. Wash away your critical views of yourself. It is everyday stress that causes you to see yourself in such a harsh light. You really are a great person!

Finish by doing something that makes you feel competent and capable. Engaging in a hobby or reading a book are good pastimes. A favorite drink and chocolate always help.

The best way to feel good about others is to start by feeling good about you.

Boudica

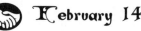

February 14
Tuesday

3rd ♎

Color of the day: Gray
Incense of the day: Ginger

Valentine's Day

Bad Love, Go Away!

It's Valentine's Day and also a waning moon. Use the moon's influence to drive away negative things that hurt you in relationships.

Buy a package of Valentine's cards—the kind kids give away in school. If you can, let the moon shine on you while you do this spell.

Write a word or phrase on each card that represents something that hurts you in love, whether it prevents new relationships from forming or it exists in a current relationship. Examples: Distrust, Jealousy, Abuse, Low Self-Esteem, or Dishonesty.

With a wand, athame, or your hand, point at the cards and say:

Valentine's Day, Valentine's Day.

Poisoned love, banished be.

Hear the truth that I do say.

From these pains, I am free.

Put the cards into a paper packet. Add salt and pepper to banish evil, then tie the packet, using thread or string, with nine knots. Wait until the new moon and throw the packet from a height (roof or bridge).

Deborah Lipp

February 15
Wednesday

3rd ♎

☽ v/c 8:54 pm

Color of the day: Yellow
Incense of the day: Honeysuckle

Lupercalia home Blessing

Today is the final day of the Roman festival Lupercalia, an ancient spring-cleaning event conducted to help avert evil in the coming season and to unlock the powers of abundance and fertility in the earth. This festival was and still is honored both in cities and rural homes all throughout the Western world.

This home blessing should be done after a home cleansing and requires only a bell. At dusk, stand at the center of your home, face the west, and ring the bell three times. Say:

By Lupercus, Faunus, and Pan,
I banish the old energy of yesteryear
and winter!

Then face the east, ring the bell three times, and say:

By Lupercus, Faunus, and Pan,
I invite riches and the abundance
of spring!

While ringing the bell and fumigating the rest of your home, move through each room chanting the second line until each room has been blessed.

Devin hunter

February 16
Thursday

3rd ♎

☽ → ♏ 1:41 am

Color of the day: Turquoise
Incense of the day: Jasmine

Let There Be Peace on Earth

It seems like every time we turn on the TV or click on a current events blog, the news is filled with reports of war. There are uncivil wars in nations around the world. Religious psychopaths are raping women and girls and killing men. Drones seem to be filling the skies. It's awful. While we can donate to agencies to feed hungry people or find homes for people who live on the streets, at the same time we need to do altar work to help heal the consciousness of our beautiful planet.

Every day of the year is a good day to sing that lovely song "Let There Be Peace on Earth," written by Jill Jackson Miller and Sy Miller in 1955. But let's rewrite the verse to remove the patriarchal slant:

With Goddess as our Mother,

Cousins all are we.

Let us meet with each other

In perfect harmony.

Barbara Ardinger

February 17
Friday

3rd ♏

☽ v/c 2:38 pm

Color of the day: Pink
Incense of the day: Mint

World Human Spirit Day

All over this earth, most of what we know about our own world is superficial, shallow, and limited. Unhappy and tragic news bombards us from all sides. Today, look to the strength of the human spirit. Make this a day to search deeper for contentedness—to wonder at our achievements, contemplate possibilities, and embrace the realization that we do not have all the answers yet. Give thanks to the higher powers for all we have and all we are.

Another way to celebrate this day might be to research forward-thinking prophets and philosophers from the past, and those who currently live among us. Light candles: white for peace, purple for spiritual awareness, and black to absorb negative energy. Then say:

I call to my higher power and the power within the candle flame.

Keep me curious and open, available and welcoming, to the blessed spirituality of all like-minded humans.

Emyme

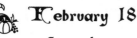

February 18
Saturday

3rd ♏

☉ → ♓ 6:31 am

☽ → ♐ 1:52 pm

4th Quarter 2:33 pm

Color of the day: Black
Incense of the day: Sandalwood

National Battery Day

Today is National Battery Day. We use batteries to power much of modern life, from flashlights to smartphones. Alas, batteries and magic don't always mix! Some magical people find that they drain batteries extra fast. Others can give a dying battery a little recharge.

On the mystical side, many things can work as a "battery" to power a spell. Quartz crystals are among the best for this purpose. A plain, clear quartz crystal can provide energy for all kinds of magical crafts. Crystals are easily recharged by putting them in sunlight or moonlight for a few hours.

Whether your favorite type of battery is technological or magical, take a few minutes to honor it today. Look at it or visualize it and say:

Vessel of power, I give thanks to you for holding the energy until it is ready to become light, motion, sound, and power.

Elizabeth Barrette

February 19
Sunday

4th ♐

Color of the day: Amber
Incense of the day: Almond

Prosperity with Every Falling Flake or Drop

This is a simple prosperity spell that you can do when it snows or rains. If you don't have some form of moisture coming from the sky on the day you want to do it, you can substitute a small pitcher and a bowl, or even confetti or glitter. The spell can be done outside or inside (looking out at the precipitation). If you are using confetti, you can do it at an altar. Take a moment to visualize each flake, droplet, or bit of confetti containing the potential for prosperity. You can even see them as gold coins. Then say:

With each flake (drop) before my eyes,

Prosperity comes from magic skies.

Falling down and all around,

Prosperity will now abound.

Deborah Blake

February 20
Monday

4th ♐

☽ v/c 6:37 pm

Color of the day: Ivory
Incense of the day: Hyssop

Presidents' Day

A Spell to Break Bad habits

Sometimes our bad habits get the best of us, and before we know it, they are running our lives and zapping our power. This spell is designed to remove the energetic ties to our bad habits and to help break the energetic cycles that they create. All you need is a piece of licorice root or, if in a pinch, a piece of black licorice candy. This spell takes advantage of the uniquely bitter flavor of licorice.

Ground and center your energy body, and visualize your bad habit and the effect it has on your life. Chew or suck on the licorice root, and after three deep breaths, say:

Bitter old habit that gets in my way,
be gone, I'm done, I've finished with
you this day!

Now visualize your life without the habit and spit the licorice into a tissue, then throw it away.

Devin hunter

February 21
Tuesday

4th ♐

☽ → ♑ 2:08 am

Color of the day: Maroon
Incense of the day: Basil

Dark Chocolate Cayenne Truffles

Spice up the passion in your relationship with this special chocolate treat. Add in the magical intent with each ingredient for a truly special candy. If you like your food only a little spicy, add half the cayenne. And if you don't like the kick at all, leave it out. You will need:

- 8 ounces dark chocolate, roughly chopped
- ½ cup heavy whipping cream
- ¼ cup powdered sugar
- 1 teaspoon vanilla extract
- 1 teaspoon ground cayenne
- ⅛ cup dark chocolate cocoa powder
- 1 teaspoon ground cinnamon

In a small, heavy-bottomed saucepan, heat the dark chocolate and cream on a medium to low heat, whisking until the chocolate is melted and the two are well mixed. Remove from heat and add the sugar, vanilla, and cayenne, whisking again until combined.

Transfer to a small bowl and refrigerate for two hours to allow it to set up and make it cool enough to handle.

In a small bowl, combine the dark chocolate cocoa powder and cinnamon. When the ganache is done cooling, roll the mixture into balls of about a tablespoon each, then roll the small balls in the cocoa/cinnamon mixture. Place on a baking sheet lined with wax paper. Store in the fridge until set. Keep refrigerated in a small, covered container.

Laurel Reufner

NOTES:

 February 22
Wednesday

4th ♑
☽ v/c 10:24 pm

Color of the day: White
Incense of the day: Lilac

Healing Spell with Quan Yin

In my father's Balinese family, Quan Yin is a deity who is venerated. She is known throughout the world as a being of deep compassion and mercy. She is also known to have originated from the mysterious bodhisattva Avalokitesvara. I have found that Quan Yin is a being who desires to be accessed by all. Go to her with respect and sincere intention and she will come to you.

Obtain an image of Quan Yin and burn jasmine or rose incense before it. Enter a state of meditation and sing the following mantra, which is dedicated to Quan Yin. As you do so, hold your intention for healing in your heart. Find a reputable source online so you can hear the mantra chanted and learn how to pronounce the words correctly:

Om mani padme hum.

Gede Parma

February 23

Thursday

4th ♑

☽ → ♒ 12:17 pm

Color of the day: Purple
Incense of the day: Apricot

Make Your Bed

Life is hectic, and it may seem like there is not enough time each morning to accomplish all you need to do before you set off for work or school or jump into your daily activities. Time may not allow for you to light a candle or stick of incense and perform a complex morning ritual or blessing. However, there is one little thing you can do that will bookend your day with self-care: make your bed.

Straighten up your sleeping room. This seemingly small act of housekeeping does wonders. Air and smooth the sheets, place decorative pillows, and open the curtains. Off you go, and what awaits you at the end of the day when you are ready to tumble into that bed? A lovely, soothing, inviting, uncluttered place to rest your body. Care for your bed and it will care for you.

Emyme

February 24

Friday

4th ♒

Color of the day: Coral
Incense of the day: Cypress

Winter's Reflection

The trees are bare. The moon casts an icy glow upon frozen landscapes. Nature has fallen into a deep sleep and nothing will stir her.

Those who dare to venture out do so quickly. Even animals appear only briefly, then return hastily to the warmth of their dens.

Yet in the stillness and quiet, we know magick stirs. Deep below the surface, life is quickening, sensing rebirth, no matter how far away it may seem.

For this spell, you will need a white candle, a quartz crystal, and a mirror.

Set the candle and crystal before the mirror. Light the candle. Hold the crystal before the candle. Allow your gaze to become soft.

As the flame reflects within the crystal, say:

Mirror bright,

Winter's night,

Crystal quartz, I see your light.

Within, without, light shines on me.

All I see is heavenly.

Najah Lightfoot

February 25

Saturday

4th ♒

☽ v/c 1:11 pm

☽ → ♓ 7:24 pm

Color of the day: Indigo
Incense of the day: Rue

Rise and Shine Oil for the Fighting Fit

Some mornings it helps to have a bit of get-up-and-go. This oil is just the trick to ease a sore back or neck, and it also relieves joint tension when used for topical pain relief.

Into one cup of liquid coconut oil, add the following pure essential oils:

- 3 drops camphor oil
- 5 drops tea tree oil
- 9 drops angelica oil
- 7 drops blue tansy oil
- 3 drops heather oil

Cover with an airtight lid and shake vigorously for thirty seconds. As you do so, imagine the spritely jigs and athletic rigors of your day, each magically being met with grace and ease. Apply the oil liberally to unbroken skin and massage in well. Avoid contact with the eyes and do not use on open cuts or wounds. For best results, store your Fighting Fit oil in the fridge and shake it vigorously before each use.

Estha McNevin

February 26

Sunday

4th ♓

New Moon 9:58 am

Color of the day: Orange
Incense of the day: Hyacinth

Solar Eclipse

The Big Reveal

Today brings a solar eclipse and a completely dark moon. This is a powerful time to work with magicks of disclosure, revealing, and beginnings, and you can do this through a simple and meaningful ritual. You'll need a candle, matches, a candle snuffer, a shawl (draped around your shoulders), a timepiece, and your favorite tarot deck.

Settle yourself about fifteen minutes before totality of the eclipse. Turn the lights out. Ground, center, and open the ritual in your usual way. Sit quietly and light the candle. As you gaze into the flame, meditate on what changes are due in your life and/or what new directions you might pursue.

When the time of the eclipse arrives, snuff the candle, pull the shawl over your head, and spend a few moments embracing the eclipsed darkness. Relight the candle, and with your meditations in mind, deal your tarot cards (use a favorite spread) and see what the universe reveals.

Susan Pesznecker

February 27
Monday

1st ♓

☽ v/c 6:08 pm

☽ → ♈ 11:52 pm

Color of the day: White
Incense of the day: Lily

Spell to Renew Good health

Do something today that is good for your health. Add new fruits or vegetables to your diet or begin an exercise program. Light a green or white candle and visualize your specific need or just focus on general well-being. If you're having trouble staying on track with a health plan such as diet or exercise, charge a piece of jewelry as you light the candle and wear it as a reminder of your goal. Chant:

As this candle burns,

Vibrant health returns.

Energy improved,

Wellness be renewed.

Allow the candle to burn out, or burn it for a few hours each day until it's spent.

Ember Grant

February 28
Tuesday

1st ♈

Color of the day: Black
Incense of the day: Cinnamon

Mardi Gras (Fat Tuesday)

Money Jar

Fat Tuesday, traditionally, is about excess. We overdo the eating and drinking before a time of abstinence. While we do not necessarily adhere to the abstinence part, we can relate to the idea of having a little extra to protect against a time of shortage.

Set up a small jar or container in which to dump pocket change in a place in your home under the watchful eyes of the gods. Allow the gods to smile down upon your efforts to ensure you have enough when the lean times come. Empty your pocket change into the jar daily or weekly and just let it accumulate.

If the jar overflows, put the money in the bank. If you find yourself short on cash, take what you need. The gods reward those who work on helping themselves. I have always found enough spare change for what I need in my money jar.

Boudica

March

March is a time of changes and a time of changelings, a time of starts and stops and renewal. This month often begins in one season and ends in another. Other months bring transitions, but March may very well bring the most radical changes. Many a blizzard has halted the commerce of a region one week of March, while sunshine and green grass and flowers overrun the week before or after.

This month being named for Mars, the god of war, means protection of self and home also figures large at this time. Ancient calendars focus on March as the start of the new year. More recently, the 15th, or the "Ides of March," brought ill fortune to Julius Caesar, and is considered by many to be unlucky. The last three days of March, long thought to be "borrowed days" of April, also call for caution. Consider doing just a little more to guard against negative energy of any sort, especially from the 10th to the 31st. A thorough house-cleaning may be in order.

In the middle of that period of caution we celebrate the vernal equinox. Ostara—the Eastern Star—is the spoke of the Wheel of the Year observed in March for earth-based believers. Paint and hide the eggs, honor the Lady with symbols of rabbits, and create your own revelry.

Emyme

March 1
Wednesday

1st ♈

☽ v/c 9:18 pm

Color of the day: Topaz
Incense of the day: Marjoram

Ash Wednesday

Wish for Something New

March seems to bring with it hope and a sense of renewal. We know winter will end soon. It's not surprising that according to the ancient Roman calendar, this was New Year's Day. This spell will bring something new into your life. You'll need the following supplies:

- A pen
- A sheet of paper
- An envelope
- A photo representing your wish
- A purple candle

First, write your wish on the paper. Then place the paper and photo in the envelope, but don't seal it yet. Next, light the candle. Gaze at the flame and visualize your wish coming true. When you feel the time is right, close the envelope and seal it by dribbling some of the warm candle wax on it. Snuff out the candle. At Ostara, open the envelope to release the spell's energy. Continue working toward your goal until you achieve your desire.

James Kambos

NOTES:

March 2
Thursday

1st ♈

☽ → ♉ 2:43 am

Color of the day: Green
Incense of the day: Clove

Personal Growth

As you explore the Pagan path, you will grow—physically, emotionally, and spiritually. But sometimes it may seem like you are getting nowhere. What did you do, where did you wander off, or did you make a wrong turn? More often than not, it is just a miscalculation and nothing serious.

The best way to track what you are doing is to keep a journal. Some call it a Book of Shadows; others call it a notepad or journal. You can blog, keep an e-file, or use a composition book and a pencil and write it all down the old-fashioned way.

When you get to a point where you are not sure about something, these references can be valuable tools in figuring out what to do next. Read where you have been, and you will see how you have grown. You will find a clue as to where you need to go next.

Boudica

March 3
Friday

1st ♉

☽ v/c 10:20 am

Color of the day: Pink
Incense of the day: Alder

house Blessing

As magickal folk, we may be called upon to cleanse or bless homes or other properties. And, of course, we can bless our own homes, too.

For this spell, you'll need a smudge stick, matches, bread, wine (or grape juice), a quartz crystal, and salt. Begin by smudging the house, first outside and then in, moving deosil (sunwise) and opening the doors and windows if possible.

Next, offer bread to the home-owner, saying:

This is so you will never be hungry.

Offer the wine:

This is so you will never thirst.

Offer the crystal:

This will fill your home with energy.

Offer the salt:

This will bring flavor to your life.

Finish with:

So shall it be!

Enjoy the bread and wine together in the freshly blessed home, scattering a few small pieces of bread and a saucer of wine outdoors for the wee folk.

Susan Pesznecker

Notes:

March 4
Saturday

1st ♉

☽ → ♊ 5:05 am

Color of the day: Gray
Incense of the day: Sage

Stillness and Quiet

In this busy world, we are constantly bombarded with stimuli. Our serenity is invaded with intrusions from our devices, our cities and towns, and our own thoughts. Sometimes we just want to run screaming, "Stop the madness, and stop this merry-go-round so I can get off!"

Even though life seems to gallop along at a frenetic pace, the world does slow down just a bit in the early morning hours, allowing us to pause and remember we are truly spiritual beings having a human experience.

This spell requires nothing more than some frankincense incense, some soft, inspiring music, and a willingness to rise before dawn.

Don't speak to anyone.
Light your incense.
Play your music.
Sit quietly as you meditate on these words:

Silence is golden, music is soothing.
My soul is renewed.

Najah Lightfoot

March 5
Sunday

1st ♊

2nd Quarter 6:32 am

Color of the day: Gold
Incense of the day: Frankincense

Multiple Personality Day

This is Multiple Personality Day. It refers to more than one soul sharing a body. Though it is often considered a disorder, it's possible for plural people to be healthy. Some cultures considered this a sign of strong magical ability, like three-in-one deities.

Closely related are aspected personalities, in which the parts of the personality are distinct yet not separate, like the facets of a crystal. Many models describe aspects of consciousness such as the "thinking self" and "primal self." People also have different roles based on work, family, and religion. It's important for those pieces to work together.

Today, light a pyramid candle with three sides. Meditate on the parts of your personality and say:

By this light I balance myself. I seek harmony within and teamwork among all the selves that I am. So mote it be.

Elizabeth Barrette

March 6
Monday

2nd ♊

☽ v/c 3:22 am

☽ → ♋ 7:54 am

Color of the day: Lavender
Incense of the day: Neroli

Meditation for March

The quiet days of winter are the perfect time to do magic that relies more on focus and inner reflection than on complicated ritual. Pick a morning or an evening when you can find a few minutes to be by yourself without interruption. Midnight is great, if you are up that late.

Sit down comfortably on a chair or cushion and light a white candle. Stare at the candle for a while, breathing slowly. Feel a sense of calm cover you like a warm blanket. If you have a question you need answered, ask it, and then wait to see if something comes to you. Otherwise, just be open to any messages the universe might have for you. Allow yourself to be silent so that you might hear your inner voice.

Deborah Blake

March 7
Tuesday

2nd ♋

Color of the day: Scarlet
Incense of the day: Ylang-ylang

Work for Justice

March 7, 1965, was "Bloody Sunday" in Selma, Alabama, a key date in the Civil Rights movement. Use today to work toward justice through peaceful means.

The Justice tarot card is ideal for this purpose. It is useful to keep a tarot deck just for spells, separate from those for readings.

Anoint a brown candle with olive oil. Light the candle, saying:

For justice.

Write your purpose on a piece of brown paper or a brown paper bag. Be specific, using only a few words, such as "passage of X bill."

Place the candle on top of the paper. Lay the Justice card before the candle, saying:

This is the outcome.
Justice will be done.

Concentrate on sending power into the candle. Repeat *Justice will be done* eight times (eight is the number of justice). When the candle has completely burned out, leave the piece of paper at a courthouse.

Deborah Lipp

March 8
Wednesday

2nd ♋

☽ v/c 9:59 am

☽ → ♌ 11:45 am

Color of the day: White
Incense of the day: Bay laurel

Breaking That Broken Record

It keeps happening. We get obsessed with something. It's undying love, eternal hate, an opinion, or a prejudice. We can't stop thinking or talking about it (or him or her). We sound like a broken record. It's time to let go.

Go to the nearest vinyl record store and buy their cheapest 78 rpm record. Light black and white candles on your altar and spend five minutes obsessing. Then say aloud:

I need to let this go. I need to be mindful. I now break this broken record.

Break the record in half, then lay the pieces on your altar and be mindful. Stop yourself from speaking or thinking about your obsession. Extinguish the candles.

The next day, light the candles again, repeat your affirmation, and break the halves in half. On the third day, repeat the affirmation and shatter each piece of the broken record. Carry one piece in your pocket to remind you to be mindful.

Barbara Ardinger

 March 9
Thursday

2nd ♌

Color of the day: Purple
Incense of the day: Myrrh

Save the Day Spell

Following a devastating brain injury, Hal Elrod created the acronym SAVERS to remember the practices he undertakes each morning that "save" the day.

S stands for silence. Get quiet in the morning: pray, meditate, breathe. Start the day in a calm state of mind.

A is for affirmations, the positive statements that encourage you toward better behavior, happy thoughts, and healthy outcomes.

V means visualization. Envision yourself doing a complex task, step by step, with a successful outcome. Focus on what success feels like.

E is for exercise. Just fifteen minutes of bodyweight exercise gets the blood flowing to the brain.

R stands for reading uplifting, inspirational material.

S is for scribing—writing down what is going on inside of you. Journaling is a great way to be in touch with your deepest desires and keep track of your progress.

Try these SAVERS to magically change your day.

Dallas Jennifer Cobb

March 10

Friday

2nd ♌

☽ v/c 12:06 pm

☽ → ♍ 5:07 pm

Color of the day: Rose

Incense of the day: Vanilla

Reiki Tag

To strengthen a psychic trust bond with someone, take some time out of your day to play a bit of Reiki tag. Sending and receiving energy is one of the essential ways that we maintain our spiritual relationships, and testing the system every now and then is a fun way to explore our compassion and understanding for others. Each person must choose three positive emotions or energies to share.

At random moments in the day, energy should be sent and received mutually. When one person initiates sharing, the other must take time out of their routine to reciprocate. Test your ability to anticipate the needs of others by looking for signs of thirst, hunger, discomfort, or emotional need. Test your observations by asking for feedback, first in person, then over the phone, and finally using only psychic skills. Discuss the results over an intimate dinner, and for the best outcome, fine-tune your trust by choosing to adapt your techniques together.

Estha McNevin

March 11

Saturday

2nd ♍

Color of the day: Black

Incense of the day: Patchouli

Persephone's Love

In the stories of Persephone, we hear of abduction and return. We read about how Demeter, Zeus, and Hades feel about and react to her. Persephone is the Sovereign Queen of the Dead and the Underworld. In my experience as her priest in this world, she is an agent of mysterious power and deep love. She chooses to pluck a strange blossom because she is curious, she desires, she dares. What of the perilous quest for love?

Take a pomegranate and hold it in your hands while in a meditative or entranced state. Project your awareness into the pomegranate. Feel its many seeds and its chambers, its hard exterior and its soft, yielding within. Know that when you burst open this fruit, you are committing to the dare of love in its infinite manifestations. This is one of the greatest risks, this dare of love. Be aware.

Gede Parma

March 12
Sunday

2nd ♏

Full Moon 10:54 am

☽ v/c 10:36 pm

Color of the day: Amber
Incense of the day: Eucalyptus

> Daylight Saving Time begins
> at 2:00 a.m. ~ Purim

Full Moon Celebration

Whether you're honoring the full moon alone or with a group, find some time to get outside and look upon her light this evening. Each month it's humbling to consider how small we are in the universe—and yet, what great things we can do. Think of those in the past who've looked upon the moon, as well as those who will see her in the future. The moon has long been a symbol and object of fascination to us. In many ways, she unites us here on Earth as we gaze up at her glowing face.

Create an altar to celebrate moonlight; use white candles, clear crystals, and silver or white decorations. Use this chant as you honor the full moon:

Brilliant moon,

We gather in the darkness as your glow arrives.

Constant moon,

Throughout the ages your presence survives.

Mirror moon,

Reflecting the light and the phases of our lives.

Ember Grant

NOTES:

March 13

Monday

3rd ♍

☽ → ♎ 1:28 am

Color of the day: Silver
Incense of the day: Rosemary

A Prayer to the Moon

As we know, the days of the week are ruled by the old gods. Monday is ruled by the moon, which is best known for its changeability. We can look up in the sky and see it every night, waxing or waning.

Sometimes we are alarmed by change. If you're facing a change that alarms you, go outside on a Monday night, contemplate the moon for a minute or two, then ask the moon or any god or goddess who rules the moon (such as Hecate, Diana, Mani, or Chandra) to prepare you for change:

Blessed (moon or goddess or god), help me understand the change I see ahead and prepare for it. As you move through your phases, you change every night, yet even when part of you is dark, you are always whole! Help me to remember that I am always whole and that change can be positive.

Barbara Ardinger

March 14

Tuesday

3rd ♎

Color of the day: Maroon
Incense of the day: Bayberry

Chaos Removal Spell

Some chaos can be a good thing, but too much can make everything in life feel insurmountable. When times feel tough and you have no direction, grab a tarot deck and cast this spell.

Remove the Wheel of Fortune and Ace of Wands cards from the deck and set the rest aside. Place the Wheel of Fortune in front of you upside down, take three deep breaths, then touch the card with your index and middle fingers and say:

Child of chaos, burning wheel of fate, bringer of darkness, bringer of hate!

Then place the Ace of Wands on top of that card, touch it with your two fingers, and say:

Child of light, burning wand of fate, bringer of light, bringer of change!

Next, place the Wheel of Fortune, right side up, on top of the Ace of Wands and say:

Chaos tamed and faith restored, a new life begins, the foundation is poured!

Devin Hunter

March 15
Wednesday

3rd ♎

☽ v/c 6:05 am

☽ → ♏ 11:11 am

Color of the day: Brown
Incense of the day: Honeysuckle

An Uplifting Spell

When heavy thoughts weigh you down, it helps to lighten up. Air magic is perfect for that purpose. This element is blithe and free, always flitting from one thing to another and generally filled with uplifting thoughts. You can harness this energy to boost your mood.

For this spell, you'll need some small symbols of air. Bells, clear crystals, wind chimes, spinners, and feathers all work well. You can also use figurines or pictures of air icons such as birds or clouds. These may be hung one at a time, strung onto cords to form long chains, or fastened together with rods to make a mobile. If you hang wind chimes or other decorations with a paddle to catch the breeze over an air vent, they will move. As you hang each one, say:

Creature of air,

So bright and fair,

Lift my thoughts on high.

East and the dawn,

Carry me on

To the happy sky.

Elizabeth Barrette

Notes:

March 16
Thursday

3rd ♏

Color of the day: Crimson
Incense of the day: Mulberry

Strong Start Plant Spell

The beginning of the growing season is almost here for many of us. Get a head start on your herbs, and give them a little magical boost. I've used this method to replant herbs, but there's no reason it wouldn't work with growing from seed as well, so feel free to use either one.

Gather your planting materials as well as some wine and a hematite stone for each pot. Fill the pot(s) halfway with your planting medium, ground yourself, and then, with intent, drop a hematite stone into the soil followed by a small pouring of the wine. As you do so, say:

Grow strong, grow full.

As the Goddess will, so may it be.

If possible, transplant outside when the weather permits.

Laurel Reufner

March 17
Friday

3rd ♏

☽ v/c 5:56 pm

☽ → ♐ 11:00 pm

Color of the day: Purple
Incense of the day: Thyme

Saint Patrick's Day

Triumph over Adversity

On this well-known holiday, let's take a different view. The story of Saint Patrick clearing the snakes out of Ireland is symbolic of his attempt to drive out the Pagans/ Celts. As we all know, he was not successful. He merely drove them underground. Perhaps this is *not* a day to celebrate Saint Patrick if one is a Pagan, and an Irish Pagan at that. Let our celebration focus instead on banished people and beliefs that did not die, but survived and strengthened over the centuries to thrive in these modern times.

Light a candle and say a prayer:

To all those forced to hide,

Now out of the dark night,

Now into the day's light,

Triumph over hate and scorn,

To flourish and be reborn.

Emyme

March 18
Saturday

3rd ♐

Color of the day: Indigo
Incense of the day: Pine

Sheela's Day

In Ireland, today is Sheela's Day, traditionally honoring Sheela-na-gig, she of the great yoni. From the Old Irish *Sile* or *Sila*, meaning "hag," Sheela is not unique to Ireland; she's been found throughout Western and Central Europe. Old and thin, she squats with her great lips hanging. A crone now, she is the mother of the world who turns the seasons, shapes the land, and sings to our souls. When there are fierce winds, storms, and wild weather, Sheela is said to be out for a walk. Come summer, she'll go to sleep on a warm rock.

Dress warmly and go out in her bluster. Turn your face into the wind or the blowing rain or snow, and see Sheela with her long white hair flowing. Whisper:

Old Hag, creator of this wonderful world, thanks for the howling winter. Time for you to rest.

Go home and toast Sheela's creations.

Dallas Jennifer Cobb

March 19
Sunday

3rd ♐

Color of the day: Yellow
Incense of the day: Marigold

Keeping Spiritually healthy

Your spiritual health is just as important as your mental and physical health. Winter tends to isolate people, keep them home, and restrict their movements.

Pagan community is really about connecting, not about being solitary. Too much emphasis is placed on solitary worship and practice. This can lead to spiritual stagnation.

Spring is just around the corner. Now would be a good time to start looking for a local Pagan community. Even in the most Pagan "unfriendly" areas, you can find spiritual fellowship. There is no reason we need to walk our path alone all the time. There are more people identifying with Paganism today than ever before, and we are easy to find.

Check at your local esoteric store or Unitarian Universalist church. The Internet can also help you locate others of like mind. Make contact and get connected!

Boudica

March 20
Monday

3rd ♐

☉ → ♈ 6:29 am

☽ v/c 6:37 am

☽ → ♑ 11:31 am

4th Quarter 11:58 am

Color of the day: White
Incense of the day: Narcissus

Spring Equinox – Ostara

Quicken Your Spirit

How we have waited for this day! The promise of spring and a new beginning has arrived. The dark days of winter are now behind us. Use the energy of Ostara and the spring equinox to quicken your spirit and renew your energy.

Gather some salt, two cups of warm water, a yellow candle, and your favorite invigorating scent (such as eucalyptus, pine, or rosemary). Take three pinches of salt and add them to the water. Anoint your candle with your scent.

Light the candle and shed your clothes. Use the saltwater to scrub your body as you stand before the flame. Invoke the spirit of spring:

Anew am I. My flesh is alive and my spirit is quickened.

Gone are the dark days.

I am renewed and reborn!

Blessed be spring!

Allow your candle to burn out safely and anoint yourself with your refreshing scent.

Najah Lightfoot

Notes:

March 21
Tuesday

4th ♑

Color of the day: Black
Incense of the day: Ginger

Prosperity Charm

With the onset of spring, life bursts from the earth and surges around us. The earth is alive with fertility and promise: it's a perfect time for prosperity magick.

You'll need a piece of green felt, a needle and thread, and a shiny new penny, nickel, dime, and quarter (include a fifty-cent piece and a silver dollar, too, if you can). Get new coins at your local bank—polish them until they shine.

Cut two identical three-inch circles from the felt. Sew them together around the edges. When mostly complete, insert the coins, then sew the pouch closed.

Holding the finished pouch over your heart, imagine and visualize your goals of prosperity, then speak your goals aloud. Keep the pouch with you, preferably next to your skin, throughout the day, and sleep with it under your pillow through the night. Then tuck it into your purse or briefcase and keep it with you until your goals materialize.

Susan Pesznecker

March 22
Wednesday

4th ♑

☽ v/c 9:20 am
☽ → ♒ 10:28 pm

Color of the day: Topaz
Incense of the day: Lilac

Spring Cleaning

At the beginning of spring, the energy of nature moves from quiet to more active. Beneath us, the earth begins to shift in subtle ways, preparing itself for growth and rebirth. Inside our homes, we can do the same thing. To prepare yourself and the place in which you live for the changes that will come with the new season, walk through your house with a smudge stick or your favorite cleansing incense (rosemary is good, or any citrus). Or you can use salt and water. As you go, say out loud:

This space is cleansed and cleared to make way for positive energy and beneficial change and growth.

If your energy feels particularly stagnant, make one pass with the smudge stick and another with the salt and water, saying your magical phrase louder and louder until you shout *So mote it be!* at the end.

Deborah Blake

March 23
Thursday

4th ♒

Color of the day: Green
Incense of the day: Nutmeg

A Shady Garden

Gardening is inherently witchy. We participate in the cycle of growth, generation, harvest, and rebirth while acquiring ingredients that can be used in spells. But not all of us have a sunny plot in which to garden.

Here are some plants that can be grown in the shade and can thrive even indoors:

Mint. Magical uses include protection of the home, healing, and drawing money. It can also be used in teas to soothe stomach problems.

Thyme. Burned, it's a purifier; under the pillow, it's a sleep aid; and carried, it promotes courage.

Woodruff. Best known as the distinct flavor in May wine, it is carried for victory and prosperity.

Angelica. The leaves, sprinkled about the house or burned in incense, are used for protection and exorcism. Avoid using the roots, which are poisonous.

Meadowsweet. Both fresh and dried, it's used in love spells. In the home, it keeps peace.

Deborah Lipp

March 24
Friday

4th ♒

Color of the day: Coral
Incense of the day: Yarrow

Family Reconciliation Spell

Sometimes family can be the worst! Sure, they can be awesome, but when they aren't, they can knock the wind right out of us. When there is tension in the family and all appears to be lost, cast this spell and avoid a high cost! All you need is a white square of paper a few inches wide, a black pen, and some honey.

Write the names of the family members involved on the piece of paper three times, rotating the paper clockwise each time a new name is to be added to the paper. Once everyone's name is on the paper, kiss the paper three times and ask for all matters to be resolved, then place it in a hole in the ground somewhere safe. Before burying it, pour the honey over the paper and say:

Love is tender, so is the heart.

Restore the family before we break apart!

Devin Hunter

March 25
Saturday

4th ≈

☽ v/c 1:56 am

☽ → ♓ 6:06 am

Color of the day: Blue
Incense of the day: Ivy

Broom Blessing

To bless a new broom or renew an old one, mix a cup of warm water with a pinch of sea salt and allow it to sit in sunlight for several hours. Add a sprinkle of lemon juice or a few drops of cedar essential oil, then sprinkle or spray the water on the broom. Visualize the broom's ability to sweep negativity from any area and to clear space for rituals or spellwork. Use this chant:

The power to cleanse, the power to clear,

To send negativity far from here;

To sweep the space and keep it clean,

Bless this broom for its magic routine.

Ember Grant

NOTES:

March 26
Sunday

4℞ ♓

Color of the day: Orange
Incense of the day: Juniper

Van Van

Get every spook and stowaway out of those dusty nooks and crannies this spring with a bit of Vodou acumen. Van Van is an antimicrobial cleaning agent that is tough on grease and grime as well as germs and allergens. Making your own can be a bit of an investment, but it's one that really saves money in the long run and also invites luck and prosperity into the home. Van Van is an all-purpose cleaner commonly used to energetically purify windows, countertops, and especially floors.

In a 32-ounce oil-safe Evo spray bottle, combine the following:

- 3 drops pure essential thyme oil
- 3 drops pure essential citronella oil
- 3 drops pure essential vervain oil
- 3 drops pure essential lemongrass oil
- 3 drops pure essential ginger oil
- 3 drops pure essential galangal oil
- 3 drops pure essential patchouli oil
- 3 drops free & clear dish soap (one with a coconut base works best)
- 5 ounces 100 proof vodka
- 5 ounces distilled white vinegar
- 22 ounces distilled water

This spray should be shaken before each use and is not safe for application on wood flooring or lacquered furnishings.

Estha McNevin

March 27
Monday

4th ♓

☽ v/c 6:19 am

☽ → ♈ 10:11 am

New Moon 10:57 pm

Color of the day: Ivory
Incense of the day: Clary sage

Dark Moon Spell of Forbidden Mysteries

There are three nights of the lunar cycle in which the moon cannot be seen in the sky. The dark moon is a time of divination, introspection, incubation, and forbidden sorceries.

In some ancient (pre-)Hellenic traditions, the dark moon period is ruled by the powers and spirits of the Underworld. Discover what the forbidden sorceries are for you.

Find an oak, yew, or cypress tree. In the evening, go to the tree and dig a small hole underneath it with your own hands. As you dig, know that you are beginning to open to your forbidden mysteries. Leave appropriate offerings that you have intuited or researched in that hole for the spirits of the below. You may trance beneath the tree. When you are finished, walk away and do not look back.

Gede Parma

March 28
Tuesday

1st ♈

Color of the day: Gray
Incense of the day: Cedar

A Spring Abundance Spell

Now that trees and shrubs are beginning to show signs of growth, it's the perfect time to perform this ritual. You'll need a pliable stem about two to three feet long from a tree or shrub such as a willow or forsythia. Begin by weaving the stem into a small wreath. As you weave, say:

The winds of winter are a thing of the past.

Spring, I welcome you at last.

Growth and abundance are drawn to me.

Now I'm blessed with prosperity.

As you weave the stem, visualize growth and abundance being bound to you. When you're done, hang the wreath on a branch of the tree or shrub from which it came. Thank the tree or shrub. You've created some positive karma, which will increase the flow of abundance coming to you.

James Kambos

March 29

Wednesday

1st ♈

☽ v/c 8:07 am

☽ → ♉ 11:48 am

Color of the day: Yellow
Incense of the day: Lavender

Unblock Your Creativity

On this day in 1848, Niagara Falls ran dry due to ice blocking the river. Personalize this day by looking inward and discovering what may be blocking you in any area of your life. No matter our profession, we all create and thus we all stumble upon an occasional block.

Start the day with a spell or blessing of your life and ask for unblocking, then be open to receive the message in any form. This may require some imagination; simply remain open in mind, heart, and spirit. Do not become discouraged, as it may take some time. Play soothing music and light your favorite scent of incense. Conjure an image of your block encased in ice. See the ice breaking apart. Creativity flows! Say:

> Blocked no more,
>
> My creativity flows
>
> Like the falls of Niagara.

Emyme

March 30

Thursday

1st ♉

☽ v/c 7:12 pm

Color of the day: Turquoise
Incense of the day: Balsam

I Affirm

Make today about personal growth and generosity by using an affirmation ritual. The repetition of an affirmation is useful to reprogram your way of thinking. You will need a journal, a special pen of your choosing, and perhaps a blue candle to burn while you work. You'll need to write your affirmation at least fifteen to twenty times a day, focusing on what you are doing. Start with something like this:

> I strive toward higher things,
> toward better things.

After three days, move on to an affirmation that focuses more specifically on what you want to work on, always using a positive *I am* or *I can* sort of statement, such as:

> I am more patient with myself.

Or perhaps:

> I am more confident when dealing
> with clients.

Give each affirmation at least a week to set in.

Laurel Reufner

March 31
Friday

1st ♉

☽ → ♊ 12:40 pm

Color of the day: White
Incense of the day: Violet

The Nurturing Log

O ak trees are sacred in Druidic tradition. Their wood is dense and strong, able to last a long time. In the forest, fallen oaks often become "nurse logs," which help new seedlings to sprout.

In the garden, logs can help retain moisture during dry times so you don't have to water your plants as often. One method is to dig a hole deep enough for the logs to rest about a foot below the surface. Another is to lay the logs on the ground and build a raised bed over them. Cover the logs with a layer of grass clippings, fill the rest of the space with soil or compost, then water thoroughly. As you work, repeat this charm:

Tree of the Druids, tree of the gods,

*Work your slow magic under
the clods.*

Hold in the water, banish the drought;

*Nourish these plants day in and
night out.*

Elizabeth Barrette

April

April is truly the deliciousness and glory of spring! In most regions, early flowers begin showing their colors as skies clear and many birds return to their homes. Humans begin spring cleanings, and everywhere, red-blooded creatures begin pairing off for the sacred dance of courtship, whether those pairings last for a lifetime or simply a few hours. This is the month of the Sacred Marriage of the Lord and the Lady, for Beltane, or May Eve, occurs at the very end of the month, on April 30th (in some traditions, it's May 1st), and Pagans everywhere begin to plan romantic and sexy activities, from private rituals involving Great Rites to large public rituals with May gads or a Maypole. Everywhere, we see couplings, new growth, fertility, and eventually, beautiful babies of all kinds.

What will you plan for your spring celebrations? Will there be May wine? It's easy to make—just throw a handful of sweet woodruff and sliced strawberries into a punch bowl with some good white wine or champagne, and let stand for the duration of your ritual. Will you plan a Maypole dance? How about a Great Rite? Whatever you choose, do it with flair and with color, and you will be honoring the glory of spring!

Thuri Calafia

April 1
Saturday

1st ♊

Color of the day: Black
Incense of the day: Sandalwood

April Fools' Day –
All Fools' Day (Pagan)

honor the Fool

The Fool, the Sacred Clown, the Trickster—this mythic figure has many names and many faces but appears in cultures around the world. Sometimes male, sometimes female, the Trickster often crosses gender lines to express some combination of both. The Trickster cracks jokes and breaks rules. Likewise, most cultures have a Day of Misrule or other occasion for turning everything upside down. All Fools' Day or April Fools' Day is one such example.

Today, honor the Fool by doing things differently than usual. You might dress in clashing colors. Try talking in Pig Latin or saying the opposite of everything you mean. Talk to people you typically ignore. Read a book or watch a movie about trickster figures. Tell stories about tricksters such as Robin Hood or Coyote. (Wile E. Coyote and the Roadrunner count too.) Have fun with it!

Don't try to do formal magic today. It will just go awry.

Elizabeth Barrette

April 2
Sunday

1st ♊

☽ v/c 10:43 am
☽ → ♋ 2:27 pm

Color of the day: Yellow
Incense of the day: Almond

Warm Communication

Today is World Autism Awareness Day. People with autism and Asperger's Syndrome often have difficulty with nonverbal communication: body language, facial expressions, etc. These steps create a magical "wand of communication."

For this spell, you will need a mercury thermometer, a piece of royal blue silk fabric, and a gray ribbon.

Place the materials on your altar. Fill yourself with images of warm, open communication. Gesture. Make faces. Laugh.

Send the energy of that communication into your materials.

Mercury is the planet of communication; its color is gray. Royal blue is the color of the fifth chakra, which rules communication. Ribbon represents being gagged, to focus the spell on the nonverbal.

Warm the thermometer in your hands. Wrap it in the silk and tie it with the ribbon. Continue to send warm, open energy into it.

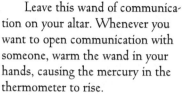

Leave this wand of communication on your altar. Whenever you want to open communication with someone, warm the wand in your hands, causing the mercury in the thermometer to rise.

Deborah Lipp

NOTES:

April 3

Monday

1st ♋

2nd Quarter 2:39 pm

Color of the day: Silver
Incense of the day: Hyssop

help Me heal

Healing can be hard. Whether it's a physical injury or an emotional imbalance, it's not easy. Add to it the stress of everyday life, and we can end up not knowing what to do next.

Medical professionals have access to all kinds of resources. They will help you if you ask them and they will see you through to the finish. Trust these people to help you with the right decisions and directions.

Life is always a mix of the mundane and the magical. As with all things, we can ask the powers that be to direct us to the right people for the help we need. Asclepius is the god of medicine and can be called upon for extra healing help. Ask for the right person to walk with you as you heal.

And be sure to ask for blessings on the people who help you.

Boudica

April 4

Tuesday

2nd ♋

☽ v/c **4:45 pm**

☽ → ♌ **6:13 pm**

Color of the day: Red
Incense of the day: Basil

Simple Stone Divination

As the days begin to grow longer and with spring finally here, it is natural to wonder what the coming year will hold. One very simple form of divination requires nothing more than a clear area outside where there are plenty of rocks or stones. Close your eyes and concentrate on what you wish to know, then ask the gods to send you a message. Say:

> In a rock let me see what my future path will be.

Then carefully walk backward until you get the feeling you should stop. Look down and find the nearest stone. Examine it for shapes and symbols that might reveal something about your future. There might be a heart or something that looks like a coin. Put the rock on your altar and look at it periodically to see if you can discern something new as time goes by.

Deborah Blake

April 5

Wednesday

2nd ♌

Color of the day: Brown
Incense of the day: Honeysuckle

help from Mercury (hermes)

The Roman Mercury (Greek Hermes, Norse Odin or Wotan), who rules Wednesday, is the god of communication, merchants, travel, and thieves. (Forget about that last one.) The planet he rules runs faster around the sun than any of his sister or brother planets. In astrology, as the messenger of the gods, Mercury rules both Gemini (talkative folks) and Virgo (detail-oriented folks). He is also known to be a wise and crafty counselor.

Wednesday is thus a good day to ask for Mercury's help and/or blessings if you're engaged in any project involving communication, selling, or travel. Start with this invocation:

> Great, swift-footed Mercury, fly to me and lend me your winged cap and winged sandals so that I may think more quickly and more clearly and move my project along more quickly.

Now explain your situation to Mercury and ask for his help or blessing.

Barbara Ardinger

April 6
Thursday

2nd ♌

☽ v/c 8:16 pm

Color of the day: Crimson
Incense of the day: Jasmine

Prosperity Hex

This little prosperity bag would be ideal to carry in your purse, briefcase, or backpack or to stash wherever else you might carry money. Or pop it in a cash drawer for added business success.

You will need:

- An 8-inch circle of plaid-printed flannel containing the color green
- A gold ribbon
- 4 whole coffee beans
- 1 teaspoon mustard seed
- 9 whole cloves
- A dollar coin
- 1 small magnet or 2 small pieces of hematite
- A gold candle

Place all of the ingredients in the middle of the fabric and tie shut with the ribbon. On your altar, light the gold candle. Holding the hex bag in your hands, envision it enveloped within the energy of your intent and recite the following:

Money I need and money I'll have,
for you will bring money to me.

Gold coins can be gotten at the bank, and you can check the birthday candles for inexpensive gold ones. Don't make your own coffee? Find a grocery store that lets you bag your own from their bulk containers and buy only a small amount.

Laurel Reufner

NOTES:

April 7
Friday

2nd ♌

☽ → ♍ 12:20 am

Color of the day: Purple
Incense of the day: Rose

An April Love Spell

April and love seem to go together. It's spring, the world is fresh, and love is in the air. If you're searching for a mate, try this love spell.

You'll need some pink fabric, two red candles with holders, and a pink ribbon. Cover a table or an altar with the fabric. Place the candles before you in the holders and light them. Then gaze at the flames and speak this charm:

Fire, fire, gift of the sun,

Bring me that special one.

Candles of red, burning together,

Bring me a love that will last forever.

Let the candles burn awhile, then gently snuff them out. When the wicks are cool, remove the candles from their holders and tie them together with the pink ribbon. Hide them in a safe place and forget about them.

James Kambos

April 8
Saturday

2nd ♍

Color of the day: Gray
Incense of the day: Rue

Elk Medicine Spell

To ensure hunting success this autumn, mentally prepare your awareness while the sun is in the sign of Aries. Make a spiritual connection to your hunting grounds and to the elk herd as it welcomes a new generation this spring.

Fill and stitch closed a hand-sewn leather pouch containing the following items:

- One elk tooth (procured from an ethical hunt)
- 2-inch patch of elk hide with fur intact (procured from an ethical hunt)
- Two 4-inch sections of cut elk bone (procured from an ethical hunt)
- 1 smoky quartz
- Pinch of wild grass
- 8 dried resins
- Pinch of sage
- Pinch of sweetgrass

Place this medicine bag at the entrance of your hunting trail for seventy-two hours. When you retrieve it, burn sage and sweetgrass to the spirits. Offer your prayers to the ancestors and ask for permission to fill your tag quota. On the way home, frequently stop to adore and photograph the land that you will hunt on. Collect any rubbish you encounter to engage your guardianship of the land.

Estha McNevin

NOTES:

 April 9

Sunday

2nd ♍

☽ v/c 4:21 am

☽ → ♎ 8:34 am

Color of the day: Gold
Incense of the day: Marigold

Palm Sunday

Celebrate Yourself!

V-I-C-T-O-R-Y, *victory, victory is our cry!*

When I was a young cheerleader, this was a favorite cheer for our local football team.

The use of palm fronds symbolizing victory is rooted in the history of the Olympic Games. Victors were awarded palm fronds as a symbol of victory in their chosen athletic competition. Today is Palm Sunday, when the fronds from the palm plant are used to symbolize victory and everlasting life. Use the power of this day to work your magick. Celebrate a recent victory or visualize overcoming a challenging situation.

Print or draw a picture of a palm frond. Then write down your achievement, or that which you seek to overcome, across your picture.

Turn the paper ninety degrees and write the word *Victory* across your words nine times. Fold the paper toward you. Bury it in your backyard or in a pretty flowerpot.

Najah Lightfoot

April 10
Monday

2nd ♎

Color of the day: White
Incense of the day: Lily

Balance Affirmation

Today, focus on restoring balance to areas of your life that may need attention. Balance is a somewhat general term—think about what it means to you and how you can apply it. Do you feel balanced emotionally, mentally, physically, and financially? Do you live in extremes? Once you've targeted your specific need, visualize what balance means in that area.

Use a double-terminated clear quartz point, if you have one. Imagine this as a symbol of balance. You can also use a yin-yang symbol or whatever else appeals to you. Charge the object of your choice with these words and carry it with you:

Keep me balanced, day to day,

To navigate and make my way.

Keep me steady, keep me true,

In every task that I pursue.

Ember Grant

April 11
Tuesday

2nd ♎
Full Moon 2:08 am
☽ v/c 2:19 pm
☽ → ♏ 6:42 pm

Color of the day: Black
Incense of the day: Cinnamon

Passover begins

Moon Magicks

It's that time again: the moon is full, filling the sky with glorious light. You're moved to participate—but how? Here are some ideas for using lunar energy.

Are you involved with a coven, grove, or other magickal group? Work with them to develop a ritual (Drawing Down the Moon, for instance) or carry out a solo ritual. Try Writing Down the Moon.

Go "moon bathing." Take a walk under the full moon, soaking in the lunar energies. If the skies are clear, you may even be able to read under the moonlight, and there's no better time to read magickal texts.

Charge your Craft tools by laying them on a silk scarf or altar cloth and allowing them to energize under the full moon. Create charged water by setting out a jar or chalice of pure water overnight.

Offer a greeting for the moon:

Hail to thee, Queen of the Night! May you fill my soul with your clearest light.
                                 Susan Pesznecker

NOTES:

April 12
Wednesday

3rd ♏

Color of the day: Topaz
Incense of the day: Lilac

Soften the Edges of Darkness

The days are getting longer, but not fast enough. In the early spring, I often find myself worrying about something unknown or unidentified—fretting without knowing why or over what. I've learned how to soften the edges of darkness and worry using this simple scribing practice. All you have to do is light candles and write.

I use beeswax candles, nontoxic and sweet-smelling. Light three or four of them in fireproof containers, enough to create a warm, pleasant glow. Enjoy the candlelight; observe how it softens the room's edges. Take notebook and pen, and write stream-of-consciousness, without stopping, until you've completed three pages. Don't stop, don't edit, and don't worry. Whatever niggling worry you may have had will be revealed by writing, and putting it down on paper will lighten the shadows inside you. It may still be dark outside, but inside darkness has softened.

                                 Dallas Jennifer Cobb

April 13
Thursday

3rd ♏

Color of the day: Turquoise
Incense of the day: Apricot

An Invocation of Balance

An equinox has come and gone and now the world is moving either into greater darkness or greater light. Has anything shifted in you in subtle or overt ways? Where is your invocation of balance required?

Light a candle of any color before you, perhaps at your indoor altar or at an outdoor shrine. Ground, center, and align. When you feel vividly present inside of the web of relationships, call out to the winds and the worlds:

Powers of the serpent winds,

Powers I call and conjure in,

I invoke for balance here,

I lay down my hurt and fear.

Perceive the flame before you open up and engulf you in a ring of holy flame. It holds you in its mighty spell. You may receive visions, intuitions, or insights. Record them in your journal.

Gede Parma

April 14
Friday

3rd ♏

☽ v/c 12:18 am
☽ → ♐ 6:27 am

Color of the day: Coral
Incense of the day: Orchid

Good Friday

Good Friday

For people of a faith other than Christian, Good Friday is nothing more than a day off of work and school. Others enjoy a quiet day of reflection into their private beliefs.

What fascinates me most is how the Christian celebration of Easter, and therefore Good Friday, was established by the cycle of the moon. In 325 CE, the First Council of Nicaea established that Easter would be held on the first Sunday after the first full moon occurring on or after the vernal equinox, our Ostara. The Pagan influence has never been completely erased from Christianity and other religions. You may choose to meditate on this and the power of ancient earth-based belief systems. Light silver and gold candles to honor the female and male energies. Say:

Lord and Lady, on this day,

Bless my efforts whatever they be.

Watch over me in work or play.

In turn I give fidelity.

Emyme

April 15
Saturday

3rd ♐

Color of the day: Indigo
Incense of the day: Sage

Spell to Spice It Up in the Boudoir

Every relationship needs a little spice when things get too vanilla. Cinnamon can help take things to a whole new level and can bring out the unnoticed elements of an otherwise bland flavor. When you are in need of a pick-me-up in the boudoir, brew a pot of coffee, but add one tablespoon of cinnamon to the fresh grounds before brewing. As the coffee brews, draw a pentacle of red fire in the air just above the coffeepot and say:

From soil to bean, shaft to stick,
bring back the fire and light the wick!

Cinnamon spice and all that's nice,
make us hot and double it twice!

Red flame rising, enchant this brew,
and help us be innocent, playful, and
true!

When the coffee is finished brewing, add your favorite extras and sit together with your significant other(s) and talk sexy. Let this special brew do the rest.

Devin Hunter

April 16
Sunday

3rd ♐

☽ v/c 2:26 pm

☽ → ♑ 7:05 pm

Color of the day: Amber
Incense of the day: Heliotrope

Easter

home Renewal

It's Easter Sunday, a day of resurrection and renewal. It's also a waning moon, a time to cause things to diminish or disappear. So let's do a simple spring-cleaning spell focused on driving out the unwanted and bringing renewal.

Make a strong tea of lavender and lemon or lemon verbena.

In each room of your home, repeat the following steps:

Go around the room counterclockwise, picking up any clutter while saying:

Unwanted be gone!
Unwanted be gone!

Feel free to change the word *unwanted* to something more specific about your life.

Put all the clutter away. Then dip a cleaning cloth into the tea. Go around the room clockwise, wiping down each surface and saying:

A new day dawns! A new day dawns!

Rinse the cleaning cloth between rooms so that it's fresh each time.

End by wiping down the front door of your home, inside and out.

Deborah Lipp

NOTES:

April 17
Monday

3rd ♑

Color of the day: Lavender
Incense of the day: Rosemary

Cleansing Spell

Water is an element of cleansing and purification. When the rain falls, it washes the air and the trees, making the world clean. Muddy water flows into creeks, where dirt settles along banks. Water evaporates from rivers and lakes, rising into the sky. So the clouds form fresh and pure, to shed the rain again.

Energy cycles much the same way. We gather it into magical artifacts to use in spellcraft. It can pick up negativity along the way. A good way to clean crystals, pentacles, and other durable magical items is to set them out in the rain for a few minutes. If it's not raining, you can use collected rainwater to rinse things, or sprinkle them with water. As you do so, say:

Spirit of water, spirit of rains,

Clean up this magic, wash away stains.

Everything pure and everything clean,

All freshened up, ready to be seen.

Elizabeth Barrette

April 18

Tuesday

3rd ♑

Color of the day: Scarlet
Incense of the day: Ginger

Passover ends

Clinch Knot Fortunes

Raid the ol' fishing tackle box or procure a fishing hook, lures, line, and weights from a local tackle shop. The size and weight of the gear chosen should pertain to your intended "catch." Creek and stream fishing lures work best for moderate money amounts; lake and tributary lures help to manifest commodity items or income; and ocean hooks with heavy line lures draw in big ticket goals like vehicle, property, or educational expenses.

Cut seven feet of fishing line. Pass one end of the line through the eye of the hook twice, leaving a seven-inch slack. Hold both the long-standing and short-slack lines parallel between two fingers. Wrap the slack line around the standing line seven times, chanting:

Our Lady of Life fulfills us.

Lastly, pass the line through the first loop and then between the slack line itself and the standing line. Pull the slack line until the loops constrict uniformly along the standing line and rest flush above the eye of the hook. Thread your fish hook with cash, accreditation paperwork, or an item that is symbolic of your goals. To finish, weave, weight, or bind up the excess line into small, uniform loops before hanging this charm in a doorway or window to lure in your prized catch.

Estha McNevin

NOTES:

April 19

Wednesday

3rd ♑

☽ v/c 5:57 am

4th Quarter 5:57 am

☽ → ♒ 6:52 am

☉ → ♉ 5:27 pm

Color of the day: White

Incense of the day: Marjoram

Block-Busting Spell

Sometimes we just need to grab a hammer and go to town on whatever it is that we find standing between us and the end of our desire. For this spell, you will need a hammer, orange ribbon, and a small piece of brick about the size of your palm.

Ground and center your energy, then hold the piece of brick in your hand and channel your feelings surrounding the block into it. Wrap the brick with the orange ribbon liberally so that there are no exposed edges and say:

I wrap this block because I'm in control.
I wrap it because I'm more powerful!

Now hit the brick three times with the hammer, breaking it into pieces, and say:

I smash you because I'm done and I
do it because I've won. Be gone, you're
banished. I haven't a care under the sun!

Throw the remains in the trash.

Devin Hunter

April 20

Thursday

4th ♒

Color of the day: Purple

Incense of the day: Clove

Seasonal Preparation

Seasons are changing and the time is right for planning. How do you wish your yard or garden to look? Is this the year you will make many changes, a few changes, or no change at all?

Begin with a spring clean-up. Rake, mow, and bag those last leaves from the fall and winter. Turn the soil and apply the fertilizer. Be gentle around those daffodils and hyacinths. When all is cleared, take a good, long look and map out where any new plants or flowers will be. Perhaps you are planting a tree this year.

Just as we humans like to be touched, so does the earth. Talk to the earth as you work, sending appreciation for the anticipated new growth. Your love and devotion will be returned. Say:

Mother Nature, Lady Gaia,

Bless the soil under my care.

My gratitude for your beauty

Is never-ending.

Emyme

April 21

Friday

4th ≈

☽ v/c 2:23 pm

☽ → ♓ 3:43 pm

Color of the day: Pink
Incense of the day: Mint

Child Activists

Today is a national holiday in Indonesia celebrating the birthday in 1879 of feminist princess Raden Adjeng Kartini, who brought reform to the school system, enabling girls and women to venture outside the home and receive an education.

Today, bless the child activists, past and present, who speak out against oppression and inequity. They push boundaries, bringing a greater quality of life to the forefront for all children. While thinking about child activists such as Malala Yousafzai (an outspoken Pakistani advocate for children's rights and female education) and Canadians Craig and Marc Kielburger (who founded Free the Children, We Day, and the Me to We movement), light a candle and bless them:

Child activists, strong and free,
they stand up to inequity.

They have brave and insistent voices,
and insist on liberty and choices.

They're like this candle, bringing light.
I bless them in their daily fight.

Bless the child activists.

Dallas Jennifer Cobb

NOTES:

April 22

Saturday

4♍ ♓

Color of the day: Brown
Incense of the day: Magnolia

Earth Day

A Grass Spell

Grasses help purify the air we breathe and they help our planet. Earth Day is a good day to perform this spell. Start by mixing a handful of grass seed with some garden soil in a clean pail or other container. Go to a wooded area near a stream or river. Bless the seed and soil by raising the pail toward the sky, then set it on the ground. Hold your hands above the seed and soil and say:

Thank you, noble grass, for helping Mother Earth and all living creatures.

Now sprinkle a bit of the grass seed mixture into the stream or river, carrying your blessing to the world. Next, sprinkle some of the seed/soil mixture on the ground as a thank-you to the earth. Lastly, save a small amount of the seed and soil for yourself to use in abundance and healing spells.

James Kambos

April 23

Sunday

4♍ ♓
☽ v/c 5:34 pm
☽ → ♈ 8:32 pm

Color of the day: Gold
Incense of the day: Almond

Freyja's Fehu Spell

The first of the Nordic runes is Freyja's. It is often transliterated as Fehu (ᚠ), and its sound is the letter *f*. Practice making that sound in the cave of your mouth. Notice your lips, the vibration, where your tongue is, and how your mouth feels when you conjure the sound.

Freyja is a goddess of fertility, magic, and oracular seership and a member of the Vanir tribe. She is sister to Freyr and the daughter of Njord.

Go into a garden, whether it is at your home or a friend's or in the center of the city. Begin to trace with your projective (or power) hand the Fehu rune in the air. Make the *f* sound and wordlessly call upon Freyja to come and bless the garden with her powers of fertility and magic. Make a shrine for her in the garden to seal the spell.

Gede Parma

April 24
Monday

4th ♈

Color of the day: Ivory
Incense of the day: Neroli

A Blessing for Our Young Women

As we consider the four stages of a woman's life—Maiden, Mother, Queen, Crone—we see that springtime is the maiden season of the year. It must be hard to be a young woman in the early years of the twenty-first century. Not only do they have to cope with the usual hormonal changes, but there are also issues around social media—keeping constantly in touch and bullying—as well as education and career choices. Consider young women you know. How can you help them in practical ways? Become a mentor.

As you're mentoring a young woman, buy beads of agate (courage, health, love, protection) and tourmaline (all colors: success, courage, friendship, grounding, love, prosperity, peace, protection) and make her a bracelet or necklace. Explain the significance of each stone. Make a similar bracelet or necklace for yourself and explain to her that the two of you are now BFF (best friends forever...well, approximately forever).

Barbara Ardinger

April 25
Tuesday

4th ♈

☽ v/c 5:53 pm
☽ → ♉ 9:56 pm

Color of the day: Gray
Incense of the day: Geranium

Fire Purging Ritual

Fire is a powerful way to encourage transformation and to banish harmful energy. Today, make way for change. Write down what you wish to purge, then fold the paper and burn it. Use an outdoor fire pit or, if indoors, use a saucepan on the stove or some other heatproof container.

As the paper is burning, visualize the fire consuming that which needs to be removed from your life. You are transformed. You will rise like a phoenix from the ashes. As the paper burns, chant:

Fire, rid me of this weight,

On this night I consummate

The change I need to be set free,

Let it be the best for me.

For good of all and harm to none,

As I will, so it be done.

When the fire is out and the ashes have cooled, collect them and either set them free upon the wind or bury them.

Ember Grant

April 26
Wednesday

4th ♉

New Moon 8:16 am

Color of the day: Yellow
Incense of the day: Lavender

Friendship Ties

Take a walk down memory lane while using friendship bracelets to help strengthen a friendship. Using stranded cotton embroidery thread, pick a color that represents you and another color to represent your friend. For the third color, you'll need a blue shade of your choosing.

Cut off about eighteen inches of thread of each color to work with. Leaving about a two-inch tail, tie the ends of the three threads together in a knot, thinking about something fun the two of you did the last time you hung out together. Now start braiding, thinking of how much you appreciate this friendship.

About every ¾ inch, tie another knot, thinking of something very specific that you appreciate about your friend. Keep braiding until you have made a total of eight knots. Add another ¾ inch of braid and then tie off the last knot. Cut off the remaining thread, leaving about a two-inch tail.

Give the braid to your friend and let them know how much you appreciate having them in your life. Your friend may either wear the bracelet or keep it somewhere special.

Laurel Reufner

NOTES:

April 27
Thursday

1st ♉

☽ v/c 9:18 pm

☽ → ♊ 9:39 pm

Color of the day: Green
Incense of the day: Carnation

Pay the Bills

We can always use some extra money, no matter what we do. Sometimes we need to get out there and push.

I like candle spells. Green candles, for our greenbacks, would be a good start for this spell. Choose a simple tapered green candle, or use a three-day or seven-day money candle. Add something to your candle that draws, like sugar or honey. Use cinnamon oil as an accelerant for your spell. Dress the candle with the oil, then place it in your working space and burn it.

It will help if you also do the mundane work. Need a temporary part-time job? Someone owe you some money? Have something you can sell? Add these to your working: look for the job, call the person who owes you, or put your item up for sale. You will be surprised at how fast this will work.

Boudica

April 28
Friday

1st ♊

Color of the day: Rose
Incense of the day: Alder

Bless Your Garden

Planting time is almost here. It's time to wake up your soil and prepare your garden. But the earth still sleeps. Although we're graced with warm days, summer is still a couple months away.

Use April's energy to awaken and revive the soil. Clear away any debris that has gathered over the winter, and lightly rake the soil. If the weather allows, take your shoes off and walk in your garden. Feel the tingle of new life preparing to sprout forth.

Face the east and raise your arms. Walk a clockwise circle as you call upon the power of nature:

Great is the golden sun and the blessed season that has begun.

Great is the moon, powerful and bright, who shines upon us through the night.

Great is the rain, which cleanses and makes us whole again.

Great is the earth, on whom we do depend!

Blessed be!

Najah Lightfoot

April 29
Saturday

1st ♊

☽ v/c 5:28 pm

☽ → ♋ 9:48 pm

Color of the day: Blue

Incense of the day: Rue

Planting Seeds

As the land around us begins to blossom in earnest, we can tap into that energy to plant the seeds for abundance in our own lives. You will need a small pot of soil, a few seeds (simple herbs or flowers that can later be used for magic are nice, but anything decorative and easy to grow will do), and a small pitcher of water. (For an added boost, you can leave the water out under a full moon.) Take a moment to visualize what abundance means to you. Then plant the seeds in the pot and say this spell as you slowly water them:

> By the power of water and the power of earth,
>
> By the power of the season's sacred dance,
>
> Let abundance be given birth
>
> And all good things my life enhance.

Every time you water your seeds, remember to focus on abundance and prosperity.

Deborah Blake

 ## April 30
Sunday

1st ♋

Color of the day: Orange

Incense of the day: Juniper

Spirit Beads

Many traditions use some sort of bead string to guide prayer or meditation, and you can do the same. You'll need a cord in a chosen color, or just use black. You'll also need a set of beads, buttons, or small items for stringing. Consider the purpose of your prayer or meditation as well as the color, shape, number, and meaning of each item.

Lay out your beads and string on a surface and work with them until you have a pleasing arrangement. Now begin stringing. Use figure-eight knots between each item. The figure eight is continuous, allowing energy to flow through the string, and its shape suggests eternity.

Finish the string with more permanent square knots. Holding the string in your hands, say:

> One bead, two bead,
>
> New lessons, I heed.

Keep the beads close for the next week, and charge them under the sun and/or moon as desired. Use them thereafter when you pray, meditate, or work ritual.

Susan Pesznecker

Anciently, in Western Europe, the year was divided in two: the dark half of the year, which begins at Samhain (October 31) and lasts until May Eve, and the light half, which begins at Beltane (May 1). The light half of the year is the more active time, when the energy of life is strong and waxing and we can look forward to the promise of summer. Since May begins one of the halves of the year, it is an initiator; similar to a cardinal zodiac sign, it shifts power to the new dynamic. The dynamic of May is one of fertility in plants and animals (including humans), birth, growth, and abundance. Of course, in the Southern Hemisphere, the opposite is true: May is the month that ushers in the dark half of the year, the time of rest, reflection, and renewal. Either way, the month of May is an important door-way into the second half of the year and a major energy shift. It is the polar opposite of its November counterpart in a beautiful dance similar to the concept of yin and yang, which is a wonderful focus for meditation.

Michael Furie

May 1
Monday

1st ♋

☽ v/c 4:23 pm

Color of the day: Gray
Incense of the day: Clary sage

Beltane

Nature's Energy Medicine

Traditionally a time for lovers to sleep outdoors, Beltane is an ideal time to rekindle your loving relationship with nature and practice "forest energy medicine." Choose a place with a grove of big trees. Take a blanket, a picnic, and lots of time.

Let go of any agenda. Be fully present to nature. Walk mindfully, aware of the majesty and the protection afforded by trees. In a private spot, spread your blanket and lie down on your back, looking deep into the beautiful sky as if staring into your lover's eyes. Remove your shoes, place your bare feet on the earth, and literally ground yourself. Breathe deeply, inhaling nature's love and exhaling stress and worry. Feel the love that nature emits. The earth surrounds and protects all living things with a natural frequency pulsation of 7.83 hertz. Feel it restore you. Be healed by nature's energy medicine.

Dallas Jennifer Cobb

May 2
Tuesday

1st ♋

☽ → ♌ 12:12 am

2nd Quarter 10:47 pm

Color of the day: Maroon
Incense of the day: Cedar

Father Mars Who Protects his People

Tuesday is ruled by Mars (Tyr or Tiw in Old English). Originally an archaic god, Mars was not a war god until he was conflated with the Greek Ares. Mars was the son of Juno, second in importance to Jupiter, and he took up arms to defend his land and his people. He created conditions in and near Rome that allowed crops to grow. If you're feeling threatened in some way, call on Mars on a Tuesday:

Great Father Mars, just as you protected your lands and people in earlier days, be present with me now and defend me from (name the threat) and keep me safe. Send your warriors to stand invisibly at my door. Send your wild animals to walk invisibly by my side. Send energy to me to help me grow stronger so that I, like you, may fight if necessary for the good of the earth.

Barbara Ardinger

May 3
Wednesday

2nd ♌

Color of the day: Topaz
Incense of the day: Bay laurel

Go Fly a Kite

Breezy spring days are great for flying a kite, and kite flying makes me think of wishes and magic. You can either make or buy your kite for this spell, but either way, you'll need paper streamers for the tail. Carefully write your wish on a streamer, attach to your kite as a tail, and find a hill, a field, or a nice stretch of park to let the kite fly. The higher it goes, the better.

Laurel Reufner

May 4
Thursday

2nd ♌

☽ v/c 12:35 am
☽ → ♍ 5:47 am

Color of the day: Turquoise
Incense of the day: Balsam

A Calming Violet Spell

Wild blue violets should be blooming now and are useful in spells for healing, calming, or sleep. Occultists and herbalists believe the blue flowers represent the sky and the foliage symbolizes the earth.

For this spell, you'll need a small bouquet of blue violets in a small vase of water and a pale blue candle in a holder. First pick the violets yourself, if possible. Violets purchased at a florist shop are a good substitute. Place the bouquet on your altar with the candle. Light the candle and relax. Then moisten a fingertip with water from the vase. Touch each temple with a drop of this water. Now extinguish the candle. At this point, meditate, lie down, or nap. When done, you should feel less stressed and more energized. If you wish, place the violets on your bedside table to ensure a restful sleep.

James Kambos

May 5

Friday

2nd ♍

Color of the day: Rose
Incense of the day: Vanilla

Cinco de Mayo

Celebrating Victory

Cinco de Mayo is a holiday that celebrates the unexpected victory of the Mexican army over the French forces at the Battle of Puebla. Many of us fight battles every day, and we need to celebrate every victory, even the small ones. This spell is a celebration of your successes, large and small, as well as an acknowledgment that we are all stronger than we think.

Light a white or yellow candle and give yourself a little celebratory gift: a flower, a piece of chocolate, or a new book, perhaps. Think of the things you have accomplished recently—they don't have to be big or special, but give yourself the credit you are due. Then say this spell in a strong voice, with feeling:

I am strong and capable!

I triumph over adversity!

I am the manifestation of deity!

I am victory personified!

Huzzah for me!

Deborah Blake

May 6

Saturday

2nd ♍

☽ v/c 8:42 am

☽ → ♎ 2:20 pm

Color of the day: Indigo
Incense of the day: Sage

Home Protection

In the tradition of Hoodoo, railroad spikes are used to nail down your property. The intention is to nail down what belongs to you and keep it safe from would-be thieves or trespassers. Use the waxing moon to increase the protective energy around your home.

For this spell, you will need:

• A railroad spike

• Olive oil or protective oil

• A flowerpot

• Potting soil

• A plant

• A white candle

Anoint your candle and railroad spike with your protective oil. Fill your pot with soil.

Add your plant to the pot. Light your candle and carefully pass the railroad spike through the flame. Bury the spike vertically in the pot.

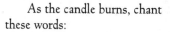

As the candle burns, chant these words:

Railroad spike, iron strong,
protect my home all year long.

Allow the candle to completely burn out, then place your protective potted plant in a conspicuous space outside your home.

Najah Lightfoot

NOTES:

May 7
Sunday

2nd ♎

Color of the day: Amber
Incense of the day: Hyacinth

Garden Blessing

When the time comes to plant your garden, a blessing is always appropriate. Whether you grow herbs, flowers, vegetables, fruit, or any combination of these, or you just have a potted plant on your windowsill, take a moment to honor the earth and ask for a successful growing season with healthy plants. This blessing can also be used when planting a tree or shrub.

One way to bless the plants (or seeds) is to sprinkle them with consecrated water. Or you can place a crystal in the soil with the plant—a clear quartz point is an ideal choice. Another option is to smudge the area by burning sage or another type of incense. Whichever method you choose, use this chant and visualize lush, vigorous growth:

Branches, buds, fruit, and seeds,

Soil, blossoms, vines, and leaves.

Bless these plants and help them grow,

On this garden strength bestow.

Ember Grant

May 8
Monday

2nd ♎

☽ v/c 6:59 pm

Color of the day: Silver
Incense of the day: Rosemary

Fire Starter

Festival season approaches! Learning to start outdoor fires "magickally" is fun and will put you in demand for rituals, festivals, and other gatherings.

Visit your local outdoor recreation store and purchase a two-piece fire-starter set. One piece is held steady while the other (the "striker") is struck sharply against the stable piece, creating sparks. The sparks then fall onto some sort of highly combustible material and voilà—fire!

Most fire starters are the traditional flint and steel. Some replace the flint component with magnesium, which yields extra-hot sparks. Practice (outdoors!) until you can create a reliable shower of sparks. Then create a pile of quick-start material to catch the sparks: fatwood shavings, shreds of newspaper, or laundry lint (from your dryer) work very well. Rehearse until you can light fire with one strike. For effect, say as you strike:

Prometheus, gift us with fire!

Susan Pesznecker

May 9
Tuesday

2nd ♎

☽ → ♏ 1:01 am

Color of the day: Red
Incense of the day: Ylang-ylang

A Project Garden Spellworking

This is a garden spell that you will work all summer. You will be growing your Project Garden. You will not be planting seeds; you will be planting projects. With the beginning of the growing season, we will make sure all our needs are in place for our plans to sprout.

Are you looking for a new job? Starting school in the fall? Projects need setup, just as seeds need soil and sun. What supplies do you need? New clothes? Books? What will be the cost of your supplies? Plan now, then find funding for your project.

Estimate the cost for what you need and burn a green candle you charge with earth energy. Then locate sources of funding, such as a summer job or a loan from a relative. Magic works best when you work with it.

Boudica

May 10
Wednesday

2nd ♏

☽ v/c 5:42 pm

Full Moon 5:42 pm

Color of the day: Yellow
Incense of the day: Honeysuckle

Sabbat Moon Spell

Many Witches and Pagans will celebrate the great feasts at the full moon nearest the calendar date. Here is a sabbat moon spell for that reason.

Beltane, the closest festival, is a fire feast, so either make a fire in your fireplace, if you have one, or light several candles in a fireproof container. If you are able to be outside, make a bonfire. Be sure to have a bucket of water or fire extinguisher nearby just in case. This spell is to call for sabbat magic to empower any spells you might be working on.

You will need a dark stone to act as a storehouse for the sabbat power. Dance around the fire and enter a trance state. Call power from the fire and the sabbat. When you reach the peak, release the power into the stone. It will hold this until you wish to transfer it into your spells.

Gede Parma

May 11

Thursday

3rd ♏

☽ → ♐ 12:59 pm

Color of the day: Purple
Incense of the day: Nutmeg

Find Your Goddess

Find a dense encyclopedia-style reference book on goddesses, such as Patricia Monaghan's *The Encyclopedia of Goddesses and Heroines*.

Light seven white candles on your altar. Remove any goddess symbols. Have the book in your lap. Ground and center. Say:

Today I find my goddess. Come to me, Lady, that I may know you.

Close your eyes. Open the book at random, allowing a spot within it to call to you. You may rifle through the pages, but your eyes should remain closed. When ready, place your finger on the spot that calls to you and open your eyes.

You've selected a goddess. Say *thank you* and extinguish the candles. Read up on the goddess you've found. What are her colors? Foods? Incenses? Rituals? Surround yourself with her sacred things and pray to her daily for a full month. Meditate on the meaning of this goddess in your life.

If, at the end of a month, you don't feel that you and she are meant to continue this relationship, you may repeat the spell.

Deborah Lipp

Notes:

May 12

Friday

3rd ♐

Color of the day: Pink
Incense of the day: Orchid

Limerick Day

It's the end of the work week, and whatever your Friday rituals or spellwork, why not use the poetry form of the limerick to bring in some humor?

The creator of the limerick is unknown. First noted after 1820 and into the mid 1800s, this form of poem consists of five lines, rhyming *aabba*. While very popular in nursery rhymes, limericks are often quite ribald and for adults only. To prepare for the weekend, I offer the following limerick, safe for any age:

It's Friday, the weekend is nigh,

With errands and chores piled high.

If Hestia please,

Work's accomplished with ease.

What's not done? I'll turn a blind eye!

— Emyme

May 13

Saturday

3rd ♐

☽ v/c 10:14 pm

Color of the day: Blue
Incense of the day: Sandalwood

Mrs. Pots

In an old teapot, combine a photo of you and your partner, a lock of hair from both your heads, and any old love letters or items of endearment from your courtship that you've kept safe. On anniversaries or special occasions, add memorabilia to your Mrs. Pots spell and store her beneath the head of your bed.

If you experience fatigue or tribulation in your relationship, investigate the heartening memories kept warmly brewing inside of good ol' Mrs. Pots. Allow the teapot to become an item of spiritual significance to you. See it as magical and mnemonic charm, inspiring compassionate understanding actively enriched by the flow of honest communication. Spells like this are a wonderful way to foster shared family and coven values.

— Estha McNevin

May 14
Sunday

3rd ♐

☽ → ♑ 1:37 am

Color of the day: Orange
Incense of the day: Frankincense

Mother's Day

O Great Mother Sun

Apollo isn't the only deity in charge of the sun. Sun goddesses include Amaterasu, Brigid, Hathor, Rosmerta, Saule, Shapash, Sulis, and many others. When we see Mother Sun as the center of the solar system, we can perhaps see greater peace among the people who are "ruled" by the planets. When we see Mother Sun shining down upon our beautiful blue planet, we can begin to see her blessings flowing into all nations and all people, even those who acknowledge only father gods.

For Mother's Day, therefore, let us stand before our altars, upon which stand sun goddesses and symbols of sunny warmth and golden power. Say:

O Great Mother Sun, shine down upon us today. Make every day your day, our Golden Mother's Day. Shine into our hearts and minds and teach us that you give warmth and light to all of us, for we are all your children.

Barbara Ardinger

May 15
Monday

3rd ♑

Color of the day: Ivory
Incense of the day: Narcissus

Let There Be Love

Love is one of the few things in life that we can never have too much of. There are many different kinds of love, including the love of family and friends, significant others, animal companions, and, of course, the love of the Goddess and God. This spell is a message to the universe that you are open to having more love in your own life, and is an invitation to send it in the best possible forms.

Light a red, pink, or white candle. If you like, put a rose or some rose petals on your altar, or a piece of rose quartz. This spell can be said for as many days in a row as feels right, or whenever you need it:

Friends and lovers, pets and kin,

With open heart I welcome in

All the love that's positive

To brighten up the life I live.

Deborah Blake

May 16
Tuesday

3rd ♑

☽ v/c 6:22 am

☽ → ♒ 1:50 pm

Color of the day: Black
Incense of the day: Basil

Making Witch's Salt

Witch's salt, also known as black salt, can be a powerful addition to your protective spells repertoire. It can often be purchased at Pagan and occult shops, but why do that when you can easily make your own?

For my Witch's salt, I use the following:

- 1 cup sea salt
- 3 self-igniting incense charcoals
- 1 teaspoon myrrh
- ¼ cup black pepper

Use a heat-resistant container to burn the charcoals on the salt, adding the myrrh as the coals get hot. After it is cool, stir in the pepper, being careful not to inhale it.

Sprinkle the salt around the outside of your home for protection or use it to boost your spell mixtures. *This salt is not to be used for cooking,* although you can buy food-safe black salt at cooking and health food stores.

Laurel Reufner

 May 17
Wednesday

3rd ♒

Color of the day: White
Incense of the day: Lavender

Spell to Break Self-Destructive Money Habits

Sometimes we can be our own worst enemy when it comes to finances. Use this spell to end bad money habits and change your financial vibe forever! For this spell, you will need three pennies, lemon-scented household cleaner, fresh water, and red nail polish.

Clean your pennies with the lemon-scented cleaner and fresh water. As you do so, chant:

Money, money, money! I love you, baby, this is true, but our relationship makes me sad and blue. With this lemon I take the bad away. Only the good between us shall stay!

Paint the head side of the pennies with red nail polish, and as they dry, gently blow on them and say:

Money, money, money! I love you, baby, this is true. Let's make our relationship fresh and new!

Place one penny on your altar and one in your pocket for spending, and include one in your next bank deposit.

Devin Hunter

May 18
Thursday

3rd ≈

☽ v/c 8:33 pm

4th Quarter 8:33 pm

☽ → ♓ 11:52 pm

Color of the day: Crimson
Incense of the day: Mulberry

International Museum Day

Today is International Museum Day. Museums invite us to explore the world—our past, the plants and animals around us, technology, art, and all kinds of exciting things. They act like temples for all deities of knowledge. Traveling to a museum broadens our horizons by showing us things we might not discover otherwise. Also, if you look in the gift shop, you might find some magical tools. Museum gift shops often have crystals, replicas of ancient artifacts, and other exciting things. So if you can, visit a museum today.

Before you go, say:

Lugh and Thoth, Apollo and Ganesh,

Gods of wisdom guide my journey.

Minerva and Benzaiten, Saraswati and Seshat,

Goddesses of knowledge light my path.

Place your discoveries before me

That I may embrace them today.

If you find a souvenir, bless it with these words:

Symbol of wisdom, travel with me
in my quest for enlightenment.

Elizabeth Barrette

NOTES:

May 19
Friday

4th ♓

Color of the day: Coral
Incense of the day: Thyme

A Spell for Courage

This spell is to be used as an aid to increase courage or strength. In this spell, I use zinnia seeds because in old magical lore zinnias represented strength, and this is the time of year to plant them. The zinnias you plant should be a warm color—red, orange, or yellow are recommended. Select your seeds and plant them according to the directions on the package. Speak these words of power in a firm voice as you plant:

> *Seeds that appear lifeless and dry,*
>
> *I ask that you grow, bloom, and delight my eye.*
>
> *And as you bloom beneath the sun's rays,*
>
> *My courage and strength increase to brighten my days.*

At high summer, your zinnias will stand tall and visitors to your garden will admire their beauty. But you, my magical friend, will know their real meaning.

James Kambos

May 20
Saturday

4th ♓

☉ → ♊ 4:31 pm
☽ v/c 11:39 pm

Color of the day: Gray
Incense of the day: Patchouli

Sunflower Seed Spell

Helianthus annuus (sunflower) is an apparition of the power of the sun. This spell works with this plant spirit and its seeds to cultivate success in an endeavor.

Ground, center, and align. If you are fortunate, you will be standing in a field of sunflowers, or else you will be holding the seeds. Do this at midday, and if you are able, stand directly under the sun. Begin to dance to raise the power. You may like to chant the following:

> *I raise the power, I raise the power,*
>
> *I raise it well, I raise it well,*
>
> *By these sun seeds, by these sun seeds,*
>
> *For this spell, for this spell.*

Focus your consciousness so that you see yourself having already achieved success in your endeavor. When the power naturally peaks, throw the sunflower seeds and feel that the spell's power releases into you as the seeds fall down to touch your skin.

Gede Parma

May 21

Sunday

4兆 ♓

☽ → ♈ 6:10 am

Color of the day: Yellow
Incense of the day: Marigold

Listening for Direction

Daily practices add up to great things. One small step after another takes you a long way. My most amazing accomplishments are all the culmination of something done daily over a long period of time. Twenty-five years clean and sober, parenting a healthy, happy teenager, and excellent health and wellness are all the result of showing up daily and taking that one small step.

Whether or not you currently meditate, set aside a few minutes today to sit in silence. Settle yourself cross-legged, with your back straight, neck long, and chin slightly tucked. Rest your hands on your thighs. Inhale deeply and exhale even more slowly. Repeat. Sink into relaxation. Focus on your posture and breath, coming back to them when your mind wanders off. Ask, *What do I need to know today?* And listen. Divine guidance will come to you from your own depths. Be blessed.

Dallas Jennifer Cobb

May 22

Monday

4兆 ♈

Color of the day: Lavender
Incense of the day: Neroli

Release Worry

When we think of cleansing and clearing, it's usually a physical object or a place—but how often do we try to clear ourselves of emotional baggage? Try this ritual as a kind of reset button for your emotions.

Make a list of things you've been worrying about—for example, finances, an employment situation, health concerns, relationships, etc. As you write down each worry, imagine you are setting it aside for a while. You don't have to worry about it or think about it at all—at least not until you're ready.

Fold the piece of paper and place a piece of black tourmaline on top of it. You can also use a clear quartz point. Leave this on your altar as long as you wish. Chant:

Things that cause me worry,
rest beneath this stone,

Help to ease the burden 'til I can
face it on my own.

When you feel the spell is complete, destroy the paper and cleanse the stone.

Ember Grant

May 23
Tuesday

4th ♈

☽ v/c 2:59 am

☽ → ♉ 8:33 am

Color of the day: Scarlet
Incense of the day: Cinnamon

Ladybug Love

Who doesn't delight in finding a ladybug in their garden? These mysterious little creatures evoke joy in everyone from the smallest child to the oldest adult. Ladybugs are aggressive eaters of pests, specifically aphids, which makes them a welcome addition to any garden. You can buy packets of ladybugs for your garden from any nursery or garden supply store. Just be sure to release them in the cool hours of the early morning.

Tuesdays are dedicated to the planet Mars, so they are good days for matters of passion, courage, aggression, and protection. Two of the colors associated with Tuesday are red and black, making this a great day for a ladybug blessing:

Ladybug, creature of red and black,

May your belly be full and know no lack.

Protect my garden and keep it free

From all pests, three times three!

Najah Lightfoot

May 24
Wednesday

4th ♉

☽ v/c 3:08 pm

Color of the day: Brown
Incense of the day: Marjoram

A Magickal Shield

For millennia, people have identified themselves and traced their lineages through heraldic shields, coats of arms, flags, and other symbolic creations.

Designing your own magickal shield strengthens your magickal identity and can be used for magickal workings as well. Start by making some notes: Who are you in terms of earth? Air? Fire? Water? What kinds of magick do you work with? What do you value? What symbols and numbers are significant to you? What colors?

Use a large piece of cardboard, fabric, or even plywood—with one quadrant each for earth, air, fire, and water and a central area for spirit. With paint, pens, wood burner, or your media of choice, design each section according to the notes you made. Keep revising and tweaking until your shield is finished. Bless it with salt, smudge, and pure water. Display it proudly in your sanctum, and consider using it as an altarpiece as well.

Susan Pesznecker

May 25
Thursday

4th ♉
☽ → ♊ 8:15 am
New Moon 3:44 pm
Color of the day: Green
Incense of the day: Myrrh

Tarot Postcard Oracle

For this spell, use an old tarot deck or procure one from a used bookstore. Divide the deck into trumps and pips. Artfully glue each of the twenty-two trumps onto a fitting postcard. Decorate each postcard with symbols, interpretations, and the mythic associations of the card. Be sure to include your own message on the back. Place each postcard inside of an individual envelope with two random pips, then mix up all the envelopes. Finally, hand-deliver your twenty-two oracle posts to random people you encounter throughout the weekend. Inquire with care regarding accuracy.

Estha McNevin

 May 26
Friday

1st ♊
Color of the day: Purple
Incense of the day: Rose

A Friend Spell

Nothing is better than having a good friend. Sometimes our best friend is just waiting for us to open up and let them in.

This spell works with symbols. Opening up can be symbolized by a flower bud. You also need to be comfortable with who you are. Comfort symbols can be a good chair or a pillow. And in a good friend relationship, there is talking and there is listening. Both of these require silence on the part of one person or the other.

Set up your space with these symbols: a quiet space, a comfortable chair or pillow, and a flower bud to open yourself. Work a list of values that you would look for in a friend and that a friend would find to value in you. Seek these things out when you meet people, and remember to share with them those things that you would like others to value in you.

Boudica

May 27
Saturday

1st ♊

☽ v/c 2:18 am

☽ → ♋ 7:25 am

Color of the day: Black
Incense of the day: Pine

Ramadan begins

A Magic Cup Spell

This spell will help wishes come true. You'll need:

- A coffee or tea cup with a saucer
- Saltwater
- A drop of olive oil
- A pen and paper

Wash the cup out three times with the saltwater. Then bless the cup by rubbing the olive oil around the inside of the cup. Write your wish on the paper. Fold the paper, place it inside the cup, and cover the cup with the saucer. Leave the cup and saucer on your altar until the wish comes to you. Then burn the paper. You may use the cup and saucer again for other spellwork, but only use it for magic.

James Kambos

May 28
Sunday

1st ♋

Color of the day: Gold
Incense of the day: Eucalyptus

Sierra Club

Today is the quasquicentennial of the founding of the Sierra Club. Created in the US 125 years ago by John Muir, this organization is dear to many Pagans, as it celebrates a love of the earth and nature. Protection and cleaning are also built into group activities.

The weather today is likely to be temperate no matter where you live. Contact your local Sierra Club chapter, gather your family, friends, and/or coven, and volunteer for a local cleaning/beautifying project. If that is not an option, you could take a walk in nature or putter in your own garden. Make it as complicated or as simple as you choose, keeping in mind our precious natural resources. Before and after, recite the following:

Our Earth is a finite resource,

Loaned, not owned.

Guide us in the best care of it.

Bless our efforts.

Emyme

May 29

Monday

1st ♋

☽ v/c 2:59 am

☽ → ♌ 8:12 am

Color of the day: Silver
Incense of the day: Lily

Memorial Day

Protect the Memory of the Fallen

Memorial Day began as Decoration Day after the Civil War. Today it honors everyone who died in the line of duty while serving in the armed forces. The American Legion uses poppies of red silk as a memento, often exchanging them for donations on Memorial Day.

As Pagans, we may call on gods and goddesses of war for protection or courage. We usually do this when going into a conflict—and that's all the attention these deities get. So today, make a donation and get a poppy to bring home for your altar as an offering to protect the memory of the fallen. Lay it before an icon of any martial deity and say:

> May the valiant dead
>
> Be remembered instead
>
> Of forgotten and left behind,
>
> As this flower of red,
>
> Laid at foot or at head,
>
> Brings their sacrifices to mind.

Elizabeth Barrette

May 30

Tuesday

1st ♌

Color of the day: White
Incense of the day: Geranium

Spell to Attract Beneficial Spirits

Witches are sometimes only as successful as the spirits they are working with allow them to be! Spirits can bring good luck and bad, but with this spell you can attract the former and avoid the latter. To cast this spell, all you need is a glass of fresh water and a shiny penny.

Tonight before bed, hold the glass of water at heart level and pray over it to be joined by beneficial spirits who want to work for your highest good. Put your right hand over the glass and say:

> With this water, I open the door for the best of spirits and nothing more! And if you get lost or need to pay some burdensome toll, here is a token of light from my soul.

Kiss the penny and drop it in the glass of water. Place the glass on a windowsill overnight.

Devin Hunter

May 31
Wednesday

1st ♌

☽ v/c 7:14 am

☽ → ♍ 12:16 pm

Color of the day: Topaz
Incense of the day: Lilac

Shavuot

What Is the Law?

Tonight marks the beginning of Shavuot, the Jewish festival that commemorates the giving of the Torah (the Five Books of Moses) on Mount Sinai.

Today, discover what your *own* law is and how to keep it.

Light five violet candles and burn some sage. Sit with a notepad and pen. Ground and center. Say aloud:

What is most important?

Write down the first word or words that come to mind.

Say again:

What is most important?

Again, write down, without editing, your first response.

Continue this process, breathing and centering between steps, until you have about ten items on your list. You can now put out the candles and incense—your ritual is complete.

These are your true values, *your* Commandments. Keep this list on your altar. Meditate on it regularly.

When you are troubled, go back to the list and ask yourself if you are living according to its principles.

Deborah Lipp

NOTES:

June

The month of June is named for Juno, the principal goddess of the Roman pantheon and wife of Jupiter. She is the patroness of marriage and the well-being of women. This is one reason June is the most popular month for weddings. June brings the magic of Midsummer—the summer solstice, the longest day of the year. Summer is ripe now with bird song and the pleasant buzz of evening insects. The gentleness of spring has given way to the powerful heat of summer—the full moon of June is called the Strong Sun Moon. Various cultures pay homage to sun gods this time of year. In some places summer is just getting started and the hottest months are yet to come, yet after the solstice we don't even notice the days beginning to get slightly shorter. This is the time for enjoying the splendor of summer: playful picnics and hikes through the woods, long nights beneath the stars, tending gardens and flower beds. Roadsides are a riot of color, and herbs such as St. John's wort, vervain, and yarrow can be used in herbal amulets. This is the time of year to honor the faeries—leave offerings for them of ale, milk, fruit, or bread before cutting flowers or herbs, and they may help your garden grow.

Ember Grant

June 1
Thursday

1st ♍

2nd Quarter 8:42 am

Color of the day: Purple
Incense of the day: Apricot

Healing Waters

In many places, the summer is a time when people make a pilgrimage to sacred waters for healing. Even if you don't have a sacred well or river near you, you can still do this spell. Any body of water will work, or even a yard or an indoor fountain. If necessary, use a bowl of water (leave it out under a full moon for extra oomph). Sprinkle a little water on head, heart, and abdomen, and say:

Healing waters, gift of the gods,

Wash away illness and disease.

Wash away pain and imbalance.

Wash away worry and sadness.

Cleanse and heal me.

Purify my mind, heart, and body,

And leave me healed by sacred waters.

So mote it be.

Deborah Blake

 **June 2**
Friday

2nd ♍

☽ v/c 5:48 pm

☽ → ♎ 8:04 pm

Color of the day: Pink
Incense of the day: Mint

Spell to Find the Right Home

Whether you are a traveler with your home in your suitcase or a very grounded-in-place kind of person, finding a home is essential in life.

Go to a place that fills you with joy. When you are in that place, open yourself to the limitless, to the mystery, to the deep well of possibility. You may bring divinatory tools to aid you in discerning a clear path ahead, or you might just surrender and listen and be.

In this place of joy, forge a strong magical link to that source of power and understand that this is what you are searching for in a home—this joy, this support, this radiance, this grounding, this feeling of welcome. Weave that link around you like a thread; perceive it absorb into your skin. It is done. You might be drawn to take something from the place with you.

Gede Parma

 June 3
Saturday

2nd ♎

Color of the day: Indigo
Incense of the day: Rue

harmony Spell

Any time you'd like to encourage peace and harmony in your home, neighborhood, or workplace, use this spell. If possible, light two white candles in the area. If it's your neighborhood, put the candles somewhere outside. If you're unable to use candles—due to workplace regulations, for example—use a clear quartz cluster (if you don't mind it being seen) or a small clear quartz point (if you want to keep it hidden). Use both the candle and the crystal if you wish.

Visualize the harmony you seek. Imagine a tense situation being resolved or noisy neighbors being quiet. Chant the following (for the workplace, change the last line to *Workplace be at peace*):

With goodwill do I intend

To see the harmony increase.

No disturbance to offend—

Home and neighborhood in peace.

Allow the candles to burn out completely. Leave the crystal in place as long as desired.

Ember Grant

June 4
Sunday

2nd ♎

Color of the day: Orange
Incense of the day: Heliotrope

Love Your Garden Spell

Plants are our spiritual helpers, and like us, they have feelings. Whether your garden is an acre or consists of a few pots on a terrace, your plants will flourish if you show them that you love them.

Begin by gently weeding and hoeing around your plants; plants love having their roots massaged. As you hoe, talk to your plants. Tell them how beautiful they are. Create a loving atmosphere in your garden by sprinkling some rose water about, or add a bit of rose water to your watering can.

As a gesture of gratitude, plant one basil plant in your garden. Basil is an excellent healing and protective herb. It'll protect your garden from negativity. But don't cut any leaves from this basil or harvest it. Allow it to grow so it may protect your garden. Your garden will respond even if you just say thank you!

James Kambos

June 5
Monday

2nd ♎

☽ v/c 4:57 am

☽ → ♏ 6:46 am

Color of the day: Ivory
Incense of the day: Narcissus

A Magickal Quotes Jar

Imagine a jar full of wisdom: a jar filled with quotes and inspirations to be delved into at exactly the right moment. You can create this jar!

You'll need a wide-mouth Mason jar with a lid, paper and pen, and scissors. Begin by writing down quotations, phrases, poems, invocations, prayers, or other short writings that influence your own magickal practices. After writing each one, cut the piece of paper to fit, fold it into a small shape, and add it to the jar. Consider words not just from magickal folks but perhaps also from astronomers, theologians, mythologists, and other learned people—and from you, too! For best results, add new materials to the jar regularly.

Once your jar is at least half full, dip into it when you need inspiration. You can also use it for divination: when you need a question answered, meditate on it, then pull a paper from the jar and consider how your question has been answered.

Susan Pesznecker

June 6
Tuesday

2nd ♏

☽ v/c 8:35 pm

Color of the day: Scarlet
Incense of the day: Ginger

Mindful Breath Meditation

Meditation is the art of clearing your mind and relaxing your body. It removes negative energy, stress, and distractions. It gathers your own energy toward productive ends. Meditation is a good regular practice and is especially helpful before performing spells or rituals.

Emptying the mind completely is very difficult for most people, so even though it's a famous method of meditation, it's not always the best choice. Everyone breathes, so breath meditation is an excellent starting point. Begin by noticing your breath. Concentrate on the sound of air moving. Feel what part of your body expands and contracts with each breath. Ideally your belly should move—that's deep breathing.

Breathe in through your nose and out through your mouth, counting each breath as you do so. Imagine ten breaths filling your root chakra. Then do ten breaths for your sacral chakra. Continue up to the crown chakra. Complete your meditation with a good stretch.

Elizabeth Barrette

June 7
Wednesday

2nd ♏

☽ → ♐ 6:59 pm

Color of the day: Brown
Incense of the day: Lavender

Speak to Me, My Muse

Sometimes we just can't get the creative juices flowing. I like to go to my muse for inspiration.

Euterpe is the muse of song and music. Erato is the muse of lyric poetry, while Calliope is the muse of epic poetry. Clio is the muse of history. Terpsichore is the muse of dance, while Thalia represents comic theater and Melpomene is tragic theater. Polyhymnia is the muse of hymns and Urania is the muse of astronomy.

I write, and while poetry is not exactly my forte, Clio has been a muse to me in the past. For all things there is a history, whether it is fiction or reality. If I am working ritual, Polyhmnia is the one I call on.

These muses provide us with sparks of interest and inspiration. Their fields of expertise can be expanded to fit your needs. Just whisper to them and then listen.

Boudica

June 8
Thursday

2nd ♐

Color of the day: White
Incense of the day: Carnation

Give Thanks to Jupiter

Thursday is ruled by Jupiter, king of the Roman gods, the Norse Thor, and the Greek Zeus. Along with Juno and Minerva, Jupiter was one of the great protectors of the Roman state until it adopted Christianity. In astrology, Jupiter gives us growth, plenty, and good fortune. Thursday is a day to give thanks for the good in your life.

Spend several minutes with paper and pen and make a list of ten good things in your life. Add ten more things. Then lay your list on your altar and say:

Father Jupiter, bringer of good fortune, I thank you for all the good in my life.

Read your list aloud. Read slowly and take time to consider each item on the list. Say:

Great Jupiter, be with me and bless me as long as I live.

Burn your list in a fireproof container (such as a small cauldron) and keep the ashes in the cauldron just inside your door.

Barbara Ardinger

June 9
Friday

2nd ♐

🌕 Full Moon 9:10 am

Color of the day: Rose
Incense of the day: Violet

Celebrate Yourself

Too often we get busy and forget what is most important. This morning, pause, breathe, smile, and choose to celebrate yourself. What do you like best about your body? What is your strongest character trait? What are you accomplished at? Where do you succeed? What brings you joy?

Celebrate your body by wearing your favorite clothes. Celebrate your health by making a delicious breakfast. Celebrate your success at work with a small treat packed in your lunch. Make plans for a special dinner out. Go alone to a restaurant or let someone take you and ask them to celebrate you too. As you are served, say thank you and receive nourishment. And after dinner, do something that brings you joy: go dancing, walk by the water, read a book, visit friends, or spend time in the garden.

Affirm:

I am worthy of celebrating. I celebrate my complete self.

Dallas Jennifer Cobb

June 10
Saturday

3rd ♐

☽ v/c 2:20 am

☽ → ♑ 7:36 am

Color of the day: Black
Incense of the day: Ivy

Intention Lemon Cleanser

Super-clean your kitchen or bathroom with this simple recipe. Focusing your intention on a clean, calm, healthy environment, mix one tablespoon lemon juice with ¼ cup baking soda. I use bottled lemon juice when making this, but I think that you'd get a stronger lemon scent if you used fresh lemon juice.

As many of us know, baking soda is a fairly natural, gentle abrasive. I use it to scrub my sink all the time. Lemon juice serves as an added cleanser, bringing insecticidal, antimicrobial, and deodorizing properties. Add in the focused magical intent and you've got a great cleanser.

Laurel Reufner

June 11
Sunday

3rd ♑

Color of the day: Gold
Incense of the day: Marigold

What I Did on My Summer Vacation

If the school year has not yet ended in your community, it soon will. One ritual many partake of this time of year is arranging a summer vacation getaway. It may be as elaborate as a trip to another country or as simple as a staycation in your own backyard. How about something in between? Daytrips to local amusement parks or historical sites are good options. Explore websites, rent books from your local library, and/or purchase vacation guidebooks. Be sure to include your partner/family in your decision-making.

Consider something educational for that all-important back-to-school essay. Request guidance from the appropriate sources. Water sprites assist with beach and lake activities, fire and earth gods and goddesses help with camping and hiking, and air spirits assist with plane travel.

Place some earth in a bowl next to a small bowl of water. Light a candle. Gently blow across the bowls. Bow to the elements. You are all set to begin planning.

Emyme

June 12
Monday

3rd ♑

☽ v/c 2:45 pm
☽ → ♒ 7:45 pm

Color of the day: White
Incense of the day: Hyssop

Computer Prosperity Spell

In the modern world, many of us make money by working on computers. Whether programming them, servicing them, or just using them to send information, we rely on computers a lot. This poses a challenge, because technology and magic don't get along very well. They tend to short-circuit each other.

Enter technomagic. This uses synthetic materials and energy instead of the nature-based kind. Metal, glass, plastic, and other humanmade things carry the spark of technomagic—and computers are basically the techie version of an enchanted mirror.

For this spell, you will need four golden coins. Put one under each corner of your computer, saying:

By north, south, east, and west,

Be this computer blessed.

Bring forth prosperity

And wealth—so mote it be!

When you need a little help, like if you're applying for a job online, just reach out and rub one of the coins.

Elizabeth Barrette

June 13
Tuesday

3rd ≈≈

Color of the day: Red
Incense of the day: Cedar

Bodies of Water

Yemaya, also known as Yemanjá, is the African orisha of oceans and seas. The goddess Sedna is the Alaskan goddess whose severed fingers formed the creatures of the sea.

Yemaya is the Great Mother who gave her love and protection to her children as they crossed the great water in the bowels of slave ships. To this very day, Brazilians honor her with tiny white boats set afloat on ocean waves.

Call upon the deities of your choosing with honor and respect. Use their stories to send blessings to the great waters of our planet. Without the great oceans we would not be, for we need the moist earth for our crops and food. Consider donating to a charity that protects the seas.

Najah Lightfoot

June 14
Wednesday

3rd ≈≈

Color of the day: Yellow
Incense of the day: Honeysuckle

Flag Day

An Energizing Bath

Summer is just around the corner. It's a perfect time to clear and reenergize body and soul.

Fill a bath-size tea bag with a handful of fresh or dried rosemary (for psychic support) and lavender (for inspiration), or knot the herbs into a tea towel.

Light nine candles in your bathroom, and draw a steaming hot bath. Pass the bath bag over your head nine times, saying:

With fatigue and stress behind,
may joy attend me, nine times nine.

Add the bath bag to the tub and swirl it clockwise through the water nine times, repeating the mantra. Settle into your bath. Using cupped hands, spill bathwater over your head nine times, imagining negativity being washed away and the charged waters anointing you with energy anew.

Enjoy your bath, relaxing, meditating, or reading until the water cools. Finish with a quick shower, then rub in moisturizing cream and don soft, clean pajamas. Extinguish the candles.

Susan Pesznecker

June 15
Thursday

3rd ♒

☽ v/c 1:40 am

☽ → ♓ 6:17 am

Color of the day: Turquoise
Incense of the day: Balsam

A Time-out Spell

As we arrive at this year's midpoint, it's time to take a break and think about what's really important to us. So take a time-out with this spell.

You'll need a small battery-powered clock, a sheet of paper, a pen, and a yellow candle. Darken the room and remove the battery from the clock. Let time stand still—this is time for you. Light the candle. On the sheet of paper, make a list of all the goals you've achieved so far this year and a list of those you haven't met. Don't feel guilty about not accomplishing everything. Gaze at the flame. Begin to feel empowered. Hold your paper and say:

I'll only accomplish what I can,

Without guilt, without shame.

When you feel ready, turn on the lights, open the windows, snuff out the candle, and set the clock to the correct time. Face the rest of the year feeling in control.

James Kambos

June 16
Friday

3rd ♓

Color of the day: Coral
Incense of the day: Vanilla

Love Meditation

How's your love life? If it's perfect, you're lucky. If not, use this meditation to focus on love in your life. Maybe you're seeking it or you're in a challenging relationship. That's not unusual, as relationships take a great deal of patience and strength.

Whatever your situation, meditate on your specific needs. The goal is to consider how to resolve any problems you're facing or find ways to open yourself to receiving love. Light a pink candle and sit quietly. Hold a piece of rose quartz if you have one. As you chant the following, see yourself being open to receiving insight:

Love can be a challenge, relationships take care,

Let me open up my heart with someone I can share.

Help me know the one I need, to form a bond that's true,

Let the love that's in my life endure, increase, renew.

Allow the candle to burn out.

Ember Grant

June 17
Saturday

3rd ♓

☽ v/c 7:33 am

4th Quarter 7:33 am

☽ → ♈ 1:55 pm

Color of the day: Gray
Incense of the day: Pine

honoring Loss,
Opening to Fullness

There are times in our lives when things are taken from us, when we let things go. These are also sacred times of witness. Here is a process to honor the transition from loss into fullness again.

Create a symbol and draw or paint it on black paper with white ink or chalk to represent your loss. Then draw a symbol on white paper in black color to represent opening to fullness. Enter a state of meditation and spend time gazing at and holding each of the symbols on their own, then notice how they feel in relationship to each other. Begin to allow your consciousness to shift into a trance state. There is a doorway between these symbols, or perhaps you will just know what to do or how to surrender in order for the transition to take place. Take three deep breaths of grounding and power. Burn both pieces of paper together in a heatproof container.

Gede Parma

June 18
Sunday

4th ♈

Color of the day: Orange
Incense of the day: Almond

Father's Day

Male Ancestor Prayer

On this Father's Day, honor your male ancestors with this simple yet powerful offering. You will need one white candle and a quiet space to perform this. Ground and center your energy, light the candle, and say this prayer:

With this flame, I light a torch along the road. Let it be a beacon for the fathers who built my blood and the men who made the family line. Let it be a beacon for the sons who grew up and the brothers we have lost. I light this torch to acknowledge their struggles, to appreciate their works, and to honor their memory. I light this torch to be in spirit with them once more and to walk this path together with them in hallowed breath. Blessed are the fathers who planted the seed. Blessed are the fathers who tended the crop. Blessed are the fathers who became the earth!

Devin hunter

June 19
Monday

4th ♈

☽ v/c 3:42 pm

☽ → ♉ 5:53 pm

Color of the day: Silver
Incense of the day: Lily

Juneteenth

Juneteenth, celebrated on June 19, or the third Saturday of June, commemorates the end of slavery in the United States.

Gather a variety of chains. A home improvement store like The Home Depot is helpful, or you might have some chains around the house: heavy chains meant to hold chandeliers, bike chains, jewelry chains, etc.

Take your chains out into some empty place, such as a field, a junkyard, etc. Pick up a chain and name it after something that binds you. For example: "This is a chain of guilt," or "This chain is my mother's unreasonable demands," or simply "Fear."

Throw the chain as far as you can. If you're doing this with friends, take turns. Have fun, shouting as you celebrate freedom from each chain.

Celebrate your new freedom with a traditional Juneteenth meal of barbeque.

It seems wrong to use such an important celebration just for personal and internal freedom, so top off your spell with a donation to an organization that fights injustice.

Deborah Lipp

Notes:

June 20
Tuesday

4th ♉

Color of the day: Maroon
Incense of the day: Bayberry

The Blessed Bees

There's always someone we don't like but still have to work with. This is someone on whom to use Blessed Honey and/or Blessed Venom.

Before your next contact with this person, close your eyes, and in your imagination pour a bucket of Blessed Honey over them. The sweetness will hopefully flow into all their pores and sweeten their disposition. The stickiness will also keep them too busy to annoy you while you're working together.

If you don't need a whole bucket of honey, imagine a smaller container, such as a cup or a tablespoon. If the person is still difficult, however, invoke the bees again and ask them to give the person a good, strong antibiotic shot of Blessed Venom (the product, of course, of the bees).

Barbara Ardinger

June 21
Wednesday

4th ♉

☉ → ♋ 12:24 am

☽ v/c 12:26 am

☽ → ♊ 6:44 pm

Color of the day: Topaz
Incense of the day: Bay laurel

Litha – Summer Solstice

Sprite Light

For this spell, you will need:

- A crafter's mask
- Crafter's latex-free gloves
- One clear and smooth-surfaced glass lantern
- A fairy stencil
- A fern leaf stencil
- Masking tape
- A small paintbrush
- Glass-etching liquid
- Paper towels
- A tealight candle

With mask and gloves firmly in place, fix the stencils to the lantern using masking tape. Use the paintbrush to apply an even coat of etching. Wait three minutes and apply another even coat. When you are satisfied with the results, clap, whistle, and ring bells to awaken your sprites.

Carefully remove each stencil and wipe them clean with a damp paper towel. Then reapply the etching liquid evenly in another location on the glass using the stencils. Repeat this process until your lamp is covered in a flurry of frenzied fairies.

Rinse your glass lantern in cold, soapy water and carefully towel-dry. When a tealight candle is lit inside the lantern, your fire fairies will leap to life.

Estha McNevin

NOTES:

June 22
Thursday

4t♅ ♊

Color of the day: Green
Incense of the day: Clove

The Dressing of the Altar

Periodically you should do a blessing for your altar. Take everything off it. Wash it carefully with glass cleaner and/or furniture polish, depending on the material. Wait for it to dry.

Add a light coat of magical "dressing" oil. You can buy this in many styles at a Pagan supply shop. If you want to make your own, a good carrier oil is almond oil, scented with a little oil of frankincense, benzoin, sandalwood, and myrrh. As you rub in the oil, say:

> Sweet oil, bless this altar with power and keep it pure.

Give the oil time to soak in.

Cover your altar with an altar cloth. Ideally you should have ones to match the seasons, different deities or themes, etc. One good trick is to have a reversible God/Goddess cloth. Cover the altar and say:

> Sacred cloth, shield this place from all negativity.

Return your altar tools to their places.

Elizabeth Barrette

June 23
Friday

4th ♊

☽ v/c 2:45 pm

☽ → ♋ 6:07 pm

New Moon 10:31 pm

Color of the day: Purple

Incense of the day: Yarrow

Fluff the Pillows

Summer is here, and it's time to fluff the pillows and change the sheets. It's amazing how such a simple act can refresh your mind, body, and spirit. It has been said that we spend one-third of our lives sleeping, yet sleep and nighttime rest remain elusive for many.

The essential oils of lavender and rose are uplifting, calming, and peaceful. Add several drops of each oil to a half cup of spring water and combine in a spray bottle. I like to use cobalt blue bottles, which are readily available at any natural food store.

The next time you change your sheets and pillowcases, fluff your pillows and mist your entire bed with the spray.

You can also mist yourself right before sleep to bring harmony to your dreamtime and relax your state of being.

Keep the bottle by your bedside to use whenever the need arises.

Najah Lightfoot

June 24
Saturday

1st ♋

Color of the day: Blue

Incense of the day: Sandalwood

Fairy Frolic

The bright days of summer are some of the best times to commune with the fairies. Remember that they are elemental creatures, not the cute little winged folk they are sometimes portrayed as, and always treat them with respect. If you wish to speak with the fairies, it is best to bring them a small offering or gift, such as a flower, a tiny cupcake, a small bowl of mead or milk, or anything shiny. Find a quiet space outside—a park will do if you don't have a yard—and put your gift down under a bush or tree. Sit silently, and when you feel as though you might not be alone, say:

I greet you, my fairy cousins,

And give you greetings and a gift.

I ask for your blessing

Under the summer sun.

Deborah Blake

June 25
Sunday

1st ♋

☽ v/c 2:44 pm

☽ → ♌ 6:06 pm

Color of the day: Amber
Incense of the day: Frankincense

Ramadan ends

Checking In on
Our Project Garden

Back on May 9th, we prepped and planted our Project Gardens, making sure all our projects' needs were met. We put together the basics, and hopefully we have the seeds of our projects set out. Now it's time to check in on the projects. Feed the projects water energy to make them grow. Use your emotional strengths to make the projects move forward. Keep a visual of water flowing and constantly moving and pushing your projects forward. Your heartfelt intent is vital for these projects to succeed.

Have you heard back on any of your projects? What kind of results are you getting? Do you need to follow up? Are you watering your projects to keep the flow going? Projects are just like plants: they need attention. Put your best foot forward. Smile as you make contacts. Impress people with your enthusiasm and attention to detail.

Keep that focus of achieving your project goals. Water your projects with love as they grow. Your determination is what will help you achieve your goals.

Boudica

Notes:

June 26
Monday

1st ♌

Color of the day: Lavender
Incense of the day: Rosemary

The Gift of Togetherness

Go to a dear friend's house and bring something you have cooked or made just for them. Bring it to them and let them know that you have intended this as a ritual act, as a magical intention.

Sit together and eat or speak about what you have created. Talk about your love for each other, how you met, and your favorite memories, even difficult ones.

When you feel like this communion of togetherness has come to completion, recite the following verse or something like it together:

Together we are strong.

Together we are wise.

Together we are abundant.

Together we forge love anew.

Gede Parma

June 27
Tuesday

1st ♌
☽ v/c 5:12 pm
☽ → ♍ 8:41 pm

Color of the day: Gray
Incense of the day: Basil

Rainbow of Peace

Who doesn't need a little more peace in their life, right? For this spell, you'll be making a ribbon rainbow peace wreath to hang in your home. You'll need:

- A variety of ribbons (or fabric strips) in a rainbow of colors, ranging in width from ¼ to 5/16 inch
- A 6-inch wooden embroidery hoop
- Scissors
- A ruler

My wreath had seven alternating colors of ribbon that were each cut six inches long. This gave me four complete groupings of the ribbons on the hoop.

Making the wreath is easy—simply begin knotting the ribbons around the edge of the wreath, adding the colors in the order of the rainbow. As you do so, focus your thoughts on whatever peace you wish to make manifest. Afterward, hang the wreath somewhere special. Mine is above my altar.

If you change any of the measurements, you'll need to play around with it a little bit to find what works for you.

Laurel Reufner

Notes:

 June 28
Wednesday

1st ♍

Color of the day: White
Incense of the day: Lilac

head and heart

The two great luminaries come together when the sun is in the sign of Cancer, which is ruled by the moon. The sun represents spirit, rational intellect, self-image, willpower, and action. The moon represents joy and the transrational elements of soul, heart, feelings, and subjectivity. Use a visualization to link thinking and feeling, objectivity and subjectivity, rational and transrational. When we use these pairs together, we bring the two great luminaries, sun and moon, into relationship, and together they create life-affirming brilliance.

Sit quietly with eyes closed. Envision the sun above your head. Inhale brilliance, drawing it into your skull, brain, and spinal cord and down into the nerves of your body. Picture the moon floating over your heart. Exhale, sending lunar illumination out from the heart to the blood, pulsing throughout your body with every heartbeat. Sun and moon. Head and heart. Illuminated.

Dallas Jennifer Cobb

June 29
Thursday

1st ♍

☽ v/c 4:35 pm

Color of the day: Crimson
Incense of the day: Jasmine

Spell to Bring Back Old Friends

We all have that special friend we've lost touch with. Life has a way of bringing incredible people into our lives and then sending them off in a different direction. Maintain ties with your closest friends, no matter how long it has been, with this simple spell.

Ground and center your energy and visualize yourself sitting in an empty room alone with your friend. See a cord of light move from your belly to theirs and spend a few moments stabilizing the connection by taking slow and steady breaths and visualizing the cord growing brighter.

Compose a simple message in your mind, such as *Call me!* and visualize the words becoming a blue ball of electricity. Take another deep breath and send this blue message ball down the energy cord to your friend. Visualize them receiving the energy and the spark giving them the urge to contact you.

Devin Hunter

June 30
Friday

1st ♍

☽ → ♎ 3:02 am

2nd Quarter 8:51 pm

Color of the day: Coral
Incense of the day: Cypress

A New Phase in Life

Retirement is a word that may make you jump for joy or strike fear in your heart. On a personal note, today is the day I leave full-time employment to join the ranks of the retired. I plan to garden, improve my home, write, sleep in, work out more, and hone my craft. So many possibilities lie before me.

I have been planning for this day for years. If retirement is not a dirty word to you and you have any thoughts of retirement, today may be the day to lay out more concrete plans. First, pick a date and print it on an eight-by-ten piece of paper. Place the paper over your keyboard or altar or in some prominent place where you will see it every day. Talk about it to others. Begin or continue financial planning. Remember the power of the written and spoken word. Our thoughts make our reality. Say:

Now I begin to "work" for me.

As I write, so mote it be.

Emyme

July

Oh, July… Sweet month of sun and flowers, the "Wednesday hump" of summer. In July, life is easy. The power of the Sun God is at its peak, and all is growing and flourishing, bursting from the earth as a gift of Beltane's fertility and heading inevitably toward the Mabon harvests as the Wheel makes its inexorable turns. In July, the flowers smell sweetest and the trees are the greenest as burgeoning life fuels our creativity and gifts us with long rapturous days, wild for the taking.

July is a wonderful time to care for your local faery folk. Create a small shrine for them in your yard or garden. Leave out a saucer with a bit of honey and butter—they will appreciate it, and may bless you with wisdom and joy. Keep some rue in your pocket to avoid being led astray by the faeries in one of their wilder moments!

You might also craft a protective summer herbal amulet. Gather either three or nine of the following herbs before sunrise: chamomile, clover, comfrey, ivy, lavender, mugwort, nettle, plantain, rose, rue, St. John's wort, sweet woodruff, thyme, wort, vervain, and yarrow. Dry the herbs in a cool, dark place for a few days, then crumble and use to fill a small pouch. Carry, wear, or keep your summer amulet nearby for blessings and protection.

Susan Pesznecker

July 1
Saturday

2nd ♎

Color of the day: Brown
Incense of the day: Magnolia

Looking for Love

We all want companionship in some form: the lover, the best friend, and the companion for life.

What is your idea of a perfect mate? Make your list. Do not focus on looks so much as personality, interests, and ideals. Then write down what you have to offer someone in return. Again, focus on personality, interests, and ideals.

Make a copy of the list on a piece of paper, with your companion's values on one side and your values on the other. Carefully burn the paper in your cauldron. Ask for someone who will match the values on both your lists.

Maybe you already know someone who matches your values. Have you met someone recently who may fit your list? Remember your intent, and focus on the list of values.

If you know someone who fits the bill, reintroduce yourself to them. The magic will take over from there.

Boudica

July 2
Sunday

2nd ♎

☽ v/c 9:16 am
☽ → ♏ 12:59 pm

Color of the day: Gold
Incense of the day: Eucalyptus

For Travelers

I am someone who travels frequently, and I find that as soon as I can when I arrive in a new land, I need to ground in, give offerings, and align my soul once more. I sometimes sing into the wind or go to a liminal place where I can trance into the land.

My mother once gave me a red jasper stone, which is known for bestowing luck and protection while traveling. Procure a red jasper stone and a small magic pouch. Enter a trance in your way and project your awareness to the rippling edge of the stone's spirit. Communicate your desire for luck and protection while traveling and form an agreement. You may want to pour a spirit (such as rum or whiskey) over the stone to feed and invigorate the spirit. Place the red jasper in the pouch and carry it with you as you journey.

Gede Parma

July 3
Monday

2nd ♏

Color of the day: Gray
Incense of the day: Neroli

Polar Opposites

On six small pieces of white paper, write your current struggles. Then, on six equal-sized pieces of black paper, write the things that you feel grateful for. Place each piece of paper into a molded portion of an ice cube tray. Fill each section containing white paper with cold saltwater and the sections containing black paper with warm honey water.

Enchant the spell with the following affirmation from the *Tao Te Ching*:

> There is no greater misfortune than not knowing what is good enough, no greater flaw than always wanting more and more. Whoever knows contentment is blissful at all times.

When you are ready, carefully place the tray in the freezer to chill. Later, gather the cubes in a towel and dump them on your front step. Leave them to melt in the heat of the day. Any papers that remain will provide divinatory insight revealing the predominant energy and offering spiritual confirmation.

Estha McNevin

 ## July 4
Tuesday

2nd ♏
☽ v/c 9:34 pm

Color of the day: White
Incense of the day: Cinnamon

Independence Day

Lady Liberty

The Roman goddess Libertas became Lady Liberty during the American and French Revolutions and is the subject of numerous nineteenth-century paintings. Her most famous incarnations are the bronze statue commissioned in 1855 for the top of the Capitol Building in Washington, DC, where she stands, hardly visible, to this day; and "Liberty Enlightening the World," which we commonly call the Statue of Liberty. She was a gift from France on the occasion of America's centennial. She holds a book in one arm and with her other hand raises a torch, a common symbol of truth and purification through illumination.

If you don't already own a miniature of the Statue of Liberty, buy one and set her on your altar. Before you go to your Fourth of July picnic, contemplate these words of George Washington: "Observe good faith and justice toward all nations. Cultivate peace and harmony with all."

Barbara Ardinger

July 5
Wednesday

2nd ♏

☽ → ♐ 1:08 am

Color of the day: Topaz
Incense of the day: Marjoram

Recover from Divorce

It can be very hard to heal from a divorce or separation, even when a couple knows it's right to split. Perform this spell for yourself or another.

The couple was like two peas in a pod. Find a large pea pod.

Place the pea pod on your altar. Burn lavender incense. Pray to the Goddess for healing for the couple.

Use water (water), salt (earth), incense (air), and a candle (fire) on your altar to represent the elements. Touch the pea pod to each, saying:

By (water/earth/air/fire) do I bless this couple, (names of couple).

Split the pod and take out two large peas. Consecrate one pea, touching it to each element as you say:

By (water/earth/air/fire) do I bless (name of first person). S/he is whole and alone. S/he is at peace apart from (name of second person).

Then do the same for the second pea.

Bury the peas in separate holes in the earth. Healing will be gradual—as the peas return to earth, healing will succeed.

Deborah Lipp

NOTES:

July 6
Thursday

2nd ♐

Color of the day: Turquoise
Incense of the day: Balsam

Destroy a Bad habit Spell

This spell uses the power of a July thunderstorm to help destroy a bad habit. If you know that a thunderstorm is approaching, gather these spell materials:

- A sheet of paper
- A pen
- A flowerpot or an old dish
- Some garden soil

Write your habit on the paper. Crumple the paper and tear it up. Then place the torn-up paper in the flowerpot or dish. Cover the paper with a layer of the soil. As the storm moves in closer, place the flowerpot or dish outside in an open area. Let the power of nature do the work for you.

After the storm, the soil in your flowerpot or dish should be muddy. Take the pot or dish to a secluded spot. Now you may simply dump the mud and paper on the ground, bury it, or put it in a compost pile. The habit will fade.

James Kambos

July 7
Friday

2nd ♐

☽ v/c 10:12 am
☽ → ♑ 1:45 pm

Color of the day: Purple
Incense of the day: Alder

heal a friendship

Every relationship hits a rough patch now and then, and usually those involved are able to work things out. However, it never hurts to have a little help, especially when it's a particularly difficult rough patch.

Write the name of you and your friend on a slip of paper, then rip it in two and tape the pieces back together. Place it on your altar in front of a pink candle and put a piece of rose quartz on top of the paper. State your intention of having the friendship mended, then light the candle and allow it to burn down. Pick up the phone or log in to social media and contact your friend.

Laurel Reufner

July 8
Saturday

2nd ♑

Color of the day: Blue
Incense of the day: Pine

Bathtub Renewal Spell

Sometimes life can get overwhelming and everything can seem impossible. Break the cycle of negativity, renew your spirits, and lift the fog from your vision with this bathtub renewal spell. You will need one handful each of sea salt, lavender, and hyssop, as well as a piece of red ribbon and optional candles for ambiance.

Light your candles, then tie the ribbon around your bathtub faucet and say:

Red like the root and the seat of flame,
empower the wild spirit now tame!

Draw your bath and cast the salt and herbs into the water and say:

By earth and herb and goddess waters,
I conjure now the sacred well! Mother,
renew me and break these chains. Heal
me, bless me, and lift me from hell! So
must this be!

Devin Hunter

July 9
Sunday

2nd ♑
Full Moon 12:07 am
☽ v/c 10:12 pm

Color of the day: Yellow
Incense of the day: Hyacinth

Magick in the Morning

Draw upon the energy of the full moon to bless you on your journey and help you fulfill your destiny. Step into your power. Activate your faith. Call upon the Goddess to assist you in whatever you seek to achieve. Know it. Believe it!

Gather some salt, a white candle, a white sage bundle, and a small glass or tea cup. Fill your cup or glass with about a half cup of water. Find a quiet place where you will not be disturbed.

Add three pinches of salt to the water. Turning clockwise, sprinkle the saltwater in a circle around you. Light the white candle. Pass the smudge bundle through the flame and allow the smoke to pass over and around you. Say:

Blessed moon, full and bright,

Shining in the morning light.

Light my path both day and night,

Be a guide unto me.

Three times three I thank thee.

Pinch out the candle and snuff out the sage bundle. Go forth and know that it is so.

Najah Lightfoot

NOTES:

July 10
Monday

3rd ♑

☽ → ♒ 1:35 am

Color of the day: Ivory
Incense of the day: Clary sage

Travel Safe

Many of us travel during the summer months, and it never hurts to ask for a little protection before we leave home. This is a simple spell that can be done before you set out and, if necessary, along the way as well.

Light a black candle and waft the smoke of a sage smudge wand or some rosemary incense all around you (and your vehicle, if you are using one). If you want, you can also consecrate an amulet or agate stone to carry with you, by saging it as well. Sprinkle a little water in a circle around you. Then say:

With the power of earth and air,

With the power of fire and water,

Let me be protected on my travels

And return home safely and well.

So mote it be.

Deborah Blake

July 11
Tuesday

3rd ♒

Color of the day: Red
Incense of the day: Cedar

You–A Wandmaker!

Many magick users end up buying wands from a craftsperson, but making your own need not be complicated and can be tremendously satisfying.

You'll need a piece of thumb-width wand wood (the length should extend roughly from elbow to fingertips of your dominant arm), a pocketknife, sandpaper (several grades), beeswax, and a soft cotton cloth.

Use the knife to peel the bark and remove rough spots from the wood, then begin sanding, starting with coarse sandpaper and working to fine. When the wand is satiny smooth, rub it all over with beeswax and rub in the wax with the cloth. Repeat three times. Your wand is now ready to use.

Hold the wand and feel its balance. Charge it under midday sun and full moon and consecrate it using the four elements:

A Witch's tool, giv'n from a tree,
comes to my hands, worked just for me.

Wrap the wand in a soft cloth and keep it out of direct light when not in use.

Susan Pesznecker

July 12
Wednesday

3rd ♒

☽ v/c 8:40 am
☽ → ♓ 11:51 am

Color of the day: Brown
Incense of the day: Lilac

Creating a More Magical home

Here's something to work on all year. If you haven't already done so, redecorate your home so the entire space is magical.

Start with the eastern walls and hang a picture of the sky. Put feathers and figures of birds and flying insects and witches on their brooms on eastern shelves.

In the south, put images associated with fire, such as an erupting volcano, sun wheels with red and orange ribbons, or solar deities.

Moving to the west, hang pictures of the sea and put shells and mermaids on the shelves.

Finally, hang a picture of a magnificent forest or a tall mountain on your northern wall and set little bears and reindeer and snow globes on your shelves.

Finally, call your circle or coven together and do a new house blessing for your sacred dwelling place. You will do powerful magic here. Vow that your magic will always be for good.

Barbara Ardinger

July 13
Thursday

3rd ♓

Color of the day: Green
Incense of the day: Mulberry

Inspiration Affirmation

Whatever your creative talent, use this affirmation to charge an object for inspiration. It can be used for a musical instrument, a pen, a paintbrush, a camera, etc. Use an item that either symbolizes your art or is something you actually use to express yourself.

First hold the item in your projective (dominant) hand, or, if that's not possible, hold your hand over the item. Visualize it as a way to channel your talent. See the outcome you desire.

Chant this rhyme three times:

Help me express

The gift I possess.

Let my finesse

Bring me success!

Ember Grant

July 14
Friday

3rd ♓

☽ v/c 1:00 pm

☽ → ♈ 7:52 pm

Color of the day: White
Incense of the day: Thyme

hearth Guardian Divination

In the Craft I work, it is important to discern the spirit who is responsible for the security and protection of one's hearth. Those of us who leave the hearth-hold regularly find our support in our ancestors or other familiar spirits. However, the house—the home—will gather its own unique spiritual potency, and this is the spirit of the hearth. When we move into a new home, we often cleanse, clear, and purify the dwelling and build altars and shrines to our own spirits and gods. Who is the hearth guardian?

Light a candle in what you feel is the natural center of your home. This is where you feel the life force pooling the most. Enter a state of meditation, and with your eyes in a resting state, gaze into the center of the flame. Remember to allow yourself to blink. Hold this question:

Who is the hearth guardian here?

You will gain insight as you scry.

Gede Parma

July 15
Saturday

3rd ♈

Color of the day: Black
Incense of the day: Sage

Saturn's Blessing

S aturday is named for the Lord of Karma, the planet Saturn. Saturn influences longevity, purification, and visions. Saturday is a good day to do a banishing and purification spell on your home. From your garden or the local farmers' market or grocer, get a small bundle of seasonal herbs. Lavender, rosemary, sage, and thyme all have purification qualities and are in abundance at this time of year. Immerse the herbs in a pot of cold water, letting them infuse the water energetically. While they soak, sweep and mop your home, cleaning as you usually do. Then, to spiritually cleanse, grasp the herbs and shake off the excess water. Say:

I invoke you, Saturn, Lord of Karma.
Cleanse this home of negativity.

Move systematically through your home, flicking water droplets into each corner and saying:

Herbs and water, purify, banish
negativity from this place.

Saturn, guard and sanctify, protect
my living space.

Blessed be.

Dallas Jennifer Cobb

July 16
Sunday

3rd ♈
4th Quarter 3:26 pm
☽ v/c 10:19 pm

Color of the day: Orange
Incense of the day: Almond

Sunny Firestarters

I n the height of summer, the sun burns hot overhead. This season relates to the element of fire and the time of midday. It is all about light and heat.

Magic lets us capture this energy, so we can use it as needed in times of darkness and cold. To do this, make some firestarters. Take twigs or splits of wood about as thick as your thumb and as long as your hand. Carefully use a knife to make notches so curls of wood stick out. Now melt some wax scraps in a double boiler—this is a good way to use up stubs of candles or crayons. Dip the wood into the wax and let it cool, repeating several times.

Each time you dip, say:

Power of summer, power of sun,

Power of fire, my spell's begun.

Into the wax and into the wood,

So it will kindle, just as it should.

Elizabeth Barrette

July 17
Monday

4th ♈

☽ → ♉ 1:04 am

Color of the day: Lavender
Incense of the day: Lily

Protection for a Pet

House pets can get out into the real world. An open door or broken screen, a damaged leash, a fright that made them bolt…It happens. You want to be sure that if they get out, you can recover them.

This spell is a mix of the magical and the mundane. Be sure the pet has some form of identification. The perfect solution is a microchip. Talk to your vet about this.

There are also tags. You can use a service that provides a tag with a phone number that is called and they can alert you, or your vet may provide the same service. Just make sure your pet is identifiable.

It always helps if you discuss this with your pet's protector. Most people prefer Bast for cats and Anubis for dogs. Do some research and find that special protector for your pet.

Boudica

July 18
Tuesday

4th ♉

Color of the day: Scarlet
Incense of the day: Ylang-ylang

Holey Protection

I believe that we all need a little boost of self-confidence, self-esteem, and courage at times. Sometimes all that's necessary to provide that boost is a simple, meaningful object that you can carry with you.

Finding a holey stone (a stone containing naturally created holes) has long been considered lucky, but it can also be used for protection. You'll need to find a place where you can look for your own holey stone. Good spots include stream beds, places that sell sand and gravel, or even playgrounds with gravel surfaces.

Once you've found your holey stone, cleanse it, bless it, and string it on a small chain to wear around your neck on days when you need a little help finding your courage and dealing with your fears.

Laurel Reufner

July 19
Wednesday

4th ♉

☽ v/c 2:11 am

☽ → ♊ 3:31 am

Color of the day: White
Incense of the day: Lavender

Spell to Summon New Friends

Today the Moon is in Gemini and lends us the power to bring friends, tribe, and community together regardless of where they are. Combined with the Sun in Cancer, today is also particularly good for summoning friends and tribe members you haven't met yet! This spell is one that I have used for over a decade with great success.

Go outside and face the east at dusk and open your arms as if to embrace a lover. Draw a pentacle of orange flame in the air before you and say:

> I call to the spirits who make life good
> to carry my words across the land!
> I summon a friend who is true of
> heart, who from me will never part.
> Come to me, ally, I know you are there,
> sweet these words that travel on air!
> As I will it, so must this be!

Devin Hunter

July 20
Thursday

4th ♊

Color of the day: Crimson
Incense of the day: Myrrh

heal without Surgery

Sometimes a doctor presents you with a choice: either X happens or you need surgery. This spell pushes positive energy into the better (X) outcome, while driving surgery away.

Write the positive outcome on a piece of paper, over and over, filling the paper, while concentrating on it coming to pass. Fold the paper as small as it will go. Place it in a jar filled with honey. Seal the jar tightly. Place a green candle on top of the jar, light it, and meditate on healing energy flowing into your "sweetened" intention.

Now take a knife, representing surgery. Feel today's waning-moon energy shrinking the need for surgery until it disappears. Say over and over to the knife:

> I don't need you.

Say this while wrapping the knife in a black cloth. Send the energy of diminishment into the knife. Bury it at the soonest opportunity.

Keep the green candle burning on your sweet jar until your next doctor's appointment. Keep the jar on a fireproof tile, someplace where it won't get knocked over.

Deborah Lipp

July 21
Friday

4th ♊

☽ v/c 1:41 am

☽ → ♋ 4:09 am

Color of the day: Rose
Incense of the day: Alder

Energy Boost

Life can be exhausting, and we can all use an energy boost from time to time. The next time you need a little more energy, instead of having an extra cup of coffee, try saying this spell to ask the element of fire for the gift of its power and vitality:

Fire bright and fire strong,

Give me energy all day long.

With your warm and gentle fire,

Keep me going when I tire.

Deborah Blake

NOTES:

July 22
Saturday

4th ♋

☉ → ♌ 11:15 am

Color of the day: Indigo
Incense of the day: Sandalwood

Divination for Safe Travel

For this spell, you'll need:

- Tarot cards (or your favorite divinatory tool)
- A white candle
- A small toy car, airplane, boat, etc. (depending on your mode of travel)

Shuffle and cut your tarot cards according to your usual process.

Light a white candle. Turn one tarot card to represent you on your travels; place the toy on the card. Meditate on the candlelight, imagining every stage of your trip, from start to finish.

Turn three more tarot cards, setting them on your altar in a row. The first one represents your journey to your destination, the second one your time at the destination, and the third one your trip home.

Meditate on the cards and what they may indicate. Ask for protection and guidance, invoking a guardian deity if you choose to. When finished, extinguish the candle. Tuck the toy into your luggage, where it will serve as a protective talisman. Leave the cards on your altar until you return from your trip.

Susan Pesznecker

NOTES:

 July 23
Sunday

4th ♋

☽ v/c 2:05 am

☽ → ♌ 4:34 am

New Moon 5:46 am

Color of the day: Amber
Incense of the day: Juniper

The Parking Place Word

Anyone who lives in a city knows that finding a place to park can be a challenge. In their 1988 book *Found Goddesses*, Morgan Grey and Julia Penelope found the goddess Asphalta and created this invocation:

Hail, Asphalta, full of grace:

Help me find a parking place.

Another magical aid is the Parking Place Word. It's ZZZAAAZZZ, pronounced with great vigor and force. Say this word when you turn the corner onto the street where you want to park or when you enter the parking lot. Speak aloud where you want to park, perhaps in front of a particular house or store. Be aware that while your space will almost always open up, you may have to drive around the block or go up and down a few aisles.

Just the other night, I said ZZZAAAZZZ on my cellphone to a friend who was looking for a parking spot and a space opened up right in front of her. Really!

Barbara Ardinger

July 24
Monday

1st ♌

Color of the day: Silver
Incense of the day: Narcissus

Wee Folk

Consider the wee folk who reside in and around our homes. They protect us and bring us abundance. We, in turn, offer thanks to them.

Throughout the year, collect bottle caps and small jars or boxes. Caps filled with honey or cider and containers holding small amounts of food are great treats for the wee folk. If the treats are placed outside, be sure to put them where garden tools will not damage them or be damaged. If inside, be sure to collect them after a day or two so as not to attract unwanted pests. Biodegradable materials are a must, and no iron! Also welcome are shiny objects and items we no longer need, such as a single earring, a thimble, or a scrap of pretty fabric. Adapt this spell to your own needs:

Pixies, brownies, gnomes, and sprites,

Elves, faeries, and the like,

Gratitude for all you do.

Please take this little gift for you.

Emyme

July 25
Tuesday

1st ♌

☽ v/c 5:22 am

☽ → ♍ 6:32 am

Color of the day: Gray
Incense of the day: Geranium

Success Spell

Sprinkle cinnamon and ginger on a large plate and chant:

Bring success in all I do.

Set my goal and see it through.

Next, place as many orange and yellow (or white) candles as you can on top of the spices and light them, chanting:

Bring success in all I do.

I will make a great debut.

Visualize your goal and chant:

Bring success in all I do.

Vast rewards I will accrue.

Let the candles burn out, or extinguish them when desired. Collect some of the cinnamon and ginger and sprinkle it in a discreet place that relates to your goal. You can also put the spice inside a small plastic bag that seals—this makes it easy to carry with you.

Ember Grant

 **July 26**
Wednesday

1st ♍

Color of the day: Yellow
Incense of the day: Honeysuckle

Sunburn Soothing Bath

Summer heat and light can cause sunburn amazingly fast. Even on a cloudy day, enough ultraviolet radiation may seep through to do damage. Staying in the shade helps, but the sweltering temperatures may also produce heat rash.

Soothing a sunburn requires drawing off the heat as well as treating the burn itself. For a healing bath, fill the tub with lukewarm water and add several bags of plain green tea, which contains antioxidants. Then sprinkle a few drops of lavender essential oil into the water. These herbs have cooling properties. As you soak, say:

Green tea, take the sun away.

Lavender, cool the burn.

Leave memories of the day

As toward the night I turn.

After leaving the bath, coat your skin with a moisturizing and healing lotion such as calendula and chamomile. Aloe vera gel is good for any spots that show blisters.

Elizabeth Barrette

▽ **July 27**
Thursday

1st ♈ ♏

☽ v/c 2:31 am

☽ → ♎ 11:37 am

Color of the day: Purple
Incense of the day: Clove

Greet the Dawn Invocation

Wake up and take your first breath. Arise and greet the dawn and the brand-new day with gratitude. Weather permitting, take your body and your spirit outside.

This chant invokes the power of east, south, west, north, above, and below.

Facing east, raise your arms in salutation. Say:

Hail to the golden sun and the blessed new day that has begun.

Keep your arms raised and turn clockwise.

Facing south, say:

Hail to the south.

Facing west, say:

Hail to the west.

Facing north, say:

Hail to the north.

Face the east, look to the sky, and say:

Hail to the above, queen of heaven, great Goddess whom I love.

Touch the ground and say:

Hail to the below, sacred Mother Earth.

Stand up, give yourself a hug, and say:

Hail to the divine spirit that is me, that is we.

Feel the love and power of the divine. Go forth and have a good day!

Najah Lightfoot

NOTES:

July 28
Friday

1st ♎

Color of the day: Pink
Incense of the day: Orchid

Making a Magickal Balm

For this spell, you'll need ½ cup olive oil, a small saucepan, ¼ cup fresh or dried herbs (depending on your magickal purpose), grated beeswax, a clean empty can, wax paper, and a tongue depressor.

Step one: Warm the oil in the saucepan to bathwater temperature. Add the herbs and steep for an hour over very low heat. Pour through a strainer, discarding the herbs. You've created an herbal-infused oil.

Step two: Add an inch of water to the saucepan and heat to simmering. Add about two inches of infused oil to the clean can and set the can in the water. Allow the oil to warm.

Step three: Add beeswax to the infused oil, a small amount at a time. Stir well with the tongue depressor. Place dabs on the wax paper and allow to cool, checking the balm's thickness. If too thick, add more oil; if too thin, add more beeswax.

Store in the refrigerator. Use your balm for healing, as an adjunct to trance work or astral travel, or to anoint magickal tools.

Susan Pesznecker

July 29
Saturday

1st ♎

☽ v/c 5:30 pm

☽ → ♏ 8:23 pm

Color of the day: Gray
Incense of the day: Patchouli

Tiger heart

To provide Indo-Western light and protection around your heart, procure an image or lifelike statuette of a tiger. Cleanse this with saltwater, and light a lamp to offer fire to your jungle cat's spirit. Speak freely to the archetype god of all felines, the Hindu lion king Narasimha. Request the energy and protection of a tiger to enter into your life. Take care to discuss all of the reasons that you need strength, loyalty, and ethical fortitude to embolden you.

Invite the tiger god Nalagiri to receive your prayers and help you meet your fears and failures with intrepid determination. Place your guardian in the area of your home where you spend the most time. To make a Nalagiri shrine on a designated altar, offer golden and orange flowers, saffron incense, and a lighted lamp, as needed. Henceforth, you will never walk unguarded or alone.

Estha McNevin

July 30
Sunday

1st ♏

2nd Quarter 11:23 am

Color of the day: Yellow
Incense of the day: Marigold

hamsa

With origins in ancient Near East Mesopotamia, hamsa comes from the word *khamsa*, meaning "five," as in five fingers. Hamsa is the image of the open right hand and is a symbol of the divine feminine. Historically known as the hand of Ishtar and the hand of Inanna, the hamsa has continued to be used throughout history. Christians call it the hand of Mary, Muslims the hand of Fatima, and Jews the hand of Miriam.

Draw a hamsa and post it on your door for protection. To ward off the evil eye, decorate it with the Eye of Horus. To ward off hunger or financial problems, decorate it with date palms. The hamsa also blesses, bestowing health, fertility, long life, strength, and prosperity. Even Buddha holds up his right hand in hamsa, a mudra of protection and teaching. Whenever you need protection, hold your right hand up, palm out. Hamsa.

Dallas Jennifer Cobb

July 31
Monday

2nd ♏

☽ v/c 7:10 am

Color of the day: White
Incense of the day: Rosemary

A Spell for Success

By the end of July, the sun is in Leo and nature is at its peak. This is an auspicious time to perform a spell for success. For a spell such as this, I like to use a warm, success-attracting herb such as cinnamon. This is what I do. First, write your goal or ambition in detail on a sheet of paper. Then lay a cinnamon stick in the center of the paper and wrap the paper around the cinnamon stick. Tie this bundle together with orange yarn or ribbon.

On a sunny day close to noon, take your bundle to a garden. I prefer a flower garden where flowers are blooming in bright colors. A garden where zinnias or black-eyed Susans are blooming would be perfect. Finally, bury your bundle near the flowers or simply stick it into the soil. The spell is done.

James Kambos

August

The eighth calendar month is full of the last hurrahs of summer (or winter, if you're in the Southern Hemisphere). Originally the sixth month of the Roman calendar, August was known as Sextilis until the Senate changed it to Augustus sometime around 8 BC. This was in honor of Augustus Caesar. August was full of holidays. The month started with a public festival honoring Spes, the goddess of hope, and ended with the Charisteria, a feast at which to give thanks. Most of the deities honored in August were fertility and harvest gods. The Anglo-Saxons referred to August as Weod Monath (Weed Month) or Arn-monath (Barn Month). In the Northern Hemisphere, August marks the start of the harvest season festivals, with the celebration of Lughnassad, or Lammas, on the 1st. August starts out in the constellation of Leo, a fixed fire sign, and moves into Virgo, a mutable earth sign, around the 20th. The birthstone of the month is peridot. Interesting fun fact: no other month starts on the same day of the week as August unless it's a leap year, in which case August and February start on the same day.

Laurel Reufner

August 1
Tuesday

2nd ♏

☽ → ♐ 8:01 am

Color of the day: Black
Incense of the day: Bayberry

Lammas

Lammas Feast of Friendship

Lammas is the first of three Pagan harvest festivals, often celebrated with grains, such as bread and beer. Whether or not you have a formal ritual or feast, why not take the time on this day to celebrate with your friends (Pagan or not) by breaking bread together? You can either bake some bread yourself or buy a nice fresh loaf from a supermarket or bakery. Stand in a circle with your friends and pass the bread around so that each person can tear off a little piece. Together, raise your bits of bread and say:

Friendship is the food of life! Huzzah!

Then eat.

Deborah Blake

August 2
Wednesday

2nd ♐

Color of the day: White
Incense of the day: Lilac

Tools of the Craft

In this day and age, we use smartphones, laptops, and computers to communicate, and once in a while pen and paper make an appearance. However we choose to communicate, we all desire to express ourselves clearly and concisely.

Wednesdays are dedicated to the god Mercury, swift messenger of the gods. Use today's energy to ask for his blessing upon your tools of communication. You will need:

- 3 drops cinnamon essential oil
- ¼ cup carrier oil of your choice (such as almond or apricot oil)
- An orange candle

Add the cinnamon essential oil to the carrier oil and mix well in a small container. Light the candle and rub your palms with the blended cinnamon oil. Hold your palms over your devices and say:

Great god Mercury, I call to you.
Thank you for blessing my tools
and my words.

Pinch out your candle and repeat as necessary, or every Wednesday as a ritualistic practice.

Najah Lightfoot

NOTES:

 August 3

Thursday

2nd ♐

☽ v/c 5:38 pm

☽ → ♑ 8:37 pm

Color of the day: Crimson
Incense of the day: Nutmeg

A house Blessing

The harvest season has begun, so this spell is a good way to bless your home and family. By performing this spell, you'll show your gratitude, which will draw more abundance to you. You'll need to prepare one cornbread in a square pan. A boxed cornbread mix is very acceptable. When the cornbread is done, bless the bread by making the shape of a pentagram or cross over it with your hand. Then cut it into squares, one for each family member, from oldest to youngest. Also, set aside one piece for your home. Let this piece sit out overnight. The next day, crumble this piece of cornbread outside at each corner of your home. As you do so, thank Mother Earth for blessing your home and family with her bounty.

James Kambos

August 4
Friday

2nd ℣

Color of the day: Coral
Incense of the day: Mint

Moments of Triumph Spell

The nature of success is that it builds on itself. When you study, you learn skills. When you practice, you develop your skills. That leads to small accomplishments, which feed into greater ones. By focusing on your past achievements, you raise power toward new ones.

For this spell, you will need ten pictures of yourself accomplishing things, a piece of paper or a matboard, some double-sided tape or glue, and a scrapbook sleeve or picture frame. Arrange the pictures in a pyramid, 4–3–2–1, with minor achievements on the bottom and the best at the top. As you secure each picture, say:

By the power of three times three,

All that I will shall come to be.

By the power of nine plus one,

Success shall come as it has done.

Put the completed page in your scrapbook of shadows, or put it in the picture frame and hang it over your altar. When you need a boost, use it as a mandala while meditating on success.

Elizabeth Barrette

August 5
Saturday

2nd ℣

Color of the day: Indigo
Incense of the day: Rue

Harvesting Summer

Summer is fleeting, with just a few weekends of warmth left. Where I live, many of the lakes don't warm up enough to swim in until mid-July.

Take today to fully enjoy the delicious warmth of sun and water, harvesting their warmth. Get thee to a lake, pool, pond, river, or stream. Spend your day picnicking, playing, snoozing, reading, and relaxing by the water, in the sun. Slather on sunscreen and practice reverential sunbathing. Breathe deeply, inhaling the radiant energy. Envision your body filling with glimmering white magical light. Exhale and feel your cells hum. For adequate vitamin D production, we need only ten minutes of direct sunlight on each side of the body. When you finish the front, flip over. Then go and swim. Practice the same technique, harvesting energy from the water. In seasons to come, you can tap into this energy. Close your eyes and envision the radiance of the harvested summer stored inside.

Dallas Jennifer Cobb

August 6
Sunday

2nd ♑

☽ v/c 5:22 am

☽ → ♒ 8:15 am

Color of the day: Amber

Incense of the day: Almond

Sunny Blessings

Sunday is ruled by the sun, which astrologers tell us is the "planet" that rules and reveals our way of being in the world. The sun can bring us power, which we must be sure to use wisely. Take time on a Sunday to look at yourself in the solar goddess Amaterasu's sacred mirror and examine your way of being in the world. What do you see? Do you have a sunny disposition or are you bossy and self-involved?

Light gold or yellow candles at your altar and invoke a solar deity. Solar gods include Apollo, Horus, and Balder. Several solar goddesses are given in the May 14 spell. Say:

Bright [name of solar god/dess], shine on me so I may see myself more clearly and as others see me. Enlighten me so that I may shine with the light of kindness and honesty. Help me to bring light into other lives.

Extinguish the candles by pinching out the flames (so you don't blow the energy of your spell away) and save them to use for another solar spell.

Barbara Ardinger

NOTES:

August 7
Monday

2nd ♒

Full Moon 2:11 pm

Color of the day: White
Incense of the day: Hyssop

Lunar Eclipse

Surrounded by Love

Today is a lunar eclipse, a full moon, and Tu B'Av, the Jewish festival of love. Today, bring love into your life. If you are single, bring new love. If you are in a relationship, bring a renewed awareness of the love you feel for and from your partner.

Get two bouquets of roses. Give one to your beloved. If you're single, place the bouquet on your altar as an offering.

Dress in white, representing the purity of your intentions.

Take the second bouquet to a private outdoor location, preferably where you can see the moon. Ground and center.

Take a rose from your bouquet. Place it in the east. Say:

I am surrounded by love. Love flows from me. Love flows to me.

Place the roses in a clockwise circle, repeating the verse for each rose, ending where you began. Say:

So mote it be.

Meditate in the moonlight, encircled by roses of love.

Deborah Lipp

NOTES:

August 8
Tuesday

3rd ♒︎

☽ v/c 3:07 pm

☽ → ♓︎ 5:56 pm

Color of the day: Gray
Incense of the day: Ginger

Finding Inner Peace

Sometimes we need to find a space of inner peace away from the stresses and strains of the everyday world. It can be rough out there; this is a fact. We need a calming center to recuperate.

Be sure your home is a place of calm and quiet. The loud, continuous rumbling and ear-shattering noises of the everyday world should be replaced with the quiet tones of soft music, a water fountain, or whatever makes you feel relaxed.

Smell is also important. What smell do you associate with home and relaxation? Lavender? Sandalwood? Use oils or incense.

Finally, turn off the TV and log out of Facebook. Find a book that takes you to those magical places that fill you spiritually or emotionally with happiness, or maybe that book that takes you on adventures to faraway places.

The mundane does have its magical side. All you have to do is look for it.

Boudica

August 9
Wednesday

3rd ♓︎

Color of the day: Yellow
Incense of the day: Bay laurel

Magickal Ink

What could be better for your magickal journal or Book of Shadows than writing with your own handmade ink? You'll need four to five nails, some soapy water, a small bowl, a small amount of white vinegar, four black tea bags, white glue, and an airtight glass bottle.

Soak the nails in soapy water for about half an hour. Rinse and dry. Now soak the nails in a small bowl with enough white vinegar to cover, leaving them for two days. After two days, discard the nails.

Boil four black tea bags in one cup water for ten minutes. Cool. Mix equal parts tea water and nail water. Add white glue, drop by drop, until the ink's consistency is correct. Say:

Double double, toil and trouble,

Ink take shape and cauldron bubble.

The ink may look pale but will dry black. Store in the glass bottle.

Try out your new ink, experimenting with different papers and maybe even with magickal alphabets, and perhaps reserving the ink for your most sacred writings.

Susan Pesznecker

August 10
Thursday

3rd ♓

☽ v/c 9:38 am

Color of the day: Purple
Incense of the day: Jasmine

Elemental Clearing Spell

If you are someone who works with the elements, you know that they are associated with the cardinal directions of a magic circle. Cast the circle in your own way and invoke the presence of the elements from the directions that you align them with. When you are ready, sit in the center of the circle and reach out to the circumference and begin to incant the following as you perceive the elemental powers moving around and through you, cleansing and clearing you:

Earth, water, air, and fire,

Take me deeper, take me higher.

Cleanse and clear me as I say,

Through the night and through the day.

When you feel cleansed and cleared, unravel your circle and earth the power.

Gede Parma

August 11
Friday

3rd ♓

☽ → ♈ 1:22 am

Color of the day: Pink
Incense of the day: Violet

Go Away Spell

Sometimes the attention we receive isn't healthy. Whether it's an unwanted advance from a would-be partner, a bully, a stalker, or just someone who is overly needy and stifling, it happens. While you shouldn't rely solely on magic to end the attention, there's nothing wrong with adding a spell or two to your protective arsenal.

For this spell, you'll need a white candle, an image of a peacock with its tail coverts spread in display, some pine needles or resin, a heat-safe container, and something to represent the two of you, preferably two photos. Place the photo of you in front of the candle and behind the peacock image. Then place the photo of the other person so that it faces the peacock. Behind all of this, place the heat-safe container and light the pine needles long enough to get them to smolder. Each day, for seven days, move the other person's photo farther away. Finally, discard it altogether. Although it's entirely up to you, the pine needles really only need to be lit the first night.

Laurel Reufner

August 12
Saturday

3rd ♈

Color of the day: Blue
Incense of the day: Sage

Banish Debt

Almost everyone experiences financial difficulty at some point in their lives. When you're feeling the pressure of debt, use this spell to help yourself get rid of it.

Begin by tearing bills or other statements (or copies of them) into small pieces. Place a black (or white) tealight candle in a cauldron or other heatproof container and burn the pieces. Visualize being rid of the bills. As you burn the paper, chant:

This burden is no longer mine,

Forgotten now and for all time.

Debt be gone, please set me free,

With harm to none, I banish thee.

A solution will arise; be open to it. See yourself free of the weight of the debt. Pursue all opportunities to handle it. Keep a positive attitude that all will be resolved.

Ember Grant

August 13
Sunday

3rd ♈

☽ v/c 4:01 am
☽ → ♉ 6:40 am

Color of the day: Yellow
Incense of the day: Frankincense

The Sacrament of Hecate

Today is one of the traditional feast days of Hecate, the Titanic Witch goddess of ancient Greece. In my tradition, Sacred Fires, we fill our homes with candlelight and incense smoke and chant the name of Hecate to invoke the life-changing energies of the etheric crossroads on this night. All you need is a key that is used to lock and unlock doors and that has been ritually cleansed and charged for Hecate.

Hold the key in both hands and chant Hecate, Hec-Hec-Hecate-Hec! until you feel her energy pulsing through you. Holding the key in one hand, draw a pentacle of white fire over it with your other hand and say:

Every door I lock is an action in your name. Every door I unlock is an action the same! This key, Hecate, is my link to you. Together our magic shall always be true!

Devin Hunter

August 14
Monday

3rd ☿
☽ v/c 9:15 pm
4th Quarter 9:15 pm
Color of the day: Lavender
Incense of the day: Lily

A Peridot Dream Spell

Light green peridot is one of the gems associated with August. This gem has been honored for its beauty and magical qualities for centuries. Cleopatra's "emeralds" may have actually been peridots. Magically, peridots have a reputation for warding off evil, bringing calm, and preventing nightmares. This peridot dream spell will aid in bringing peaceful sleep.

Obtain a small, uncut peridot from a gem shop. Sometimes they're sold in collections of several stones. They're inexpensive. Bless your peridot and ask it to help you with your dreamwork. Before bedtime, burn a pale green candle, and write down anything that you think may be causing you to have nightmares. Hide the paper and snuff out the candle. Place the peridot beneath your pillow. Visualize the peridot protecting you, surrounding you with a green light as you fall asleep.

James Kambos

August 15
Tuesday

4th ☿
☽ → ♊ 10:06 am
Color of the day: Maroon
Incense of the day: Cinnamon

Transition Time

We're between Lammas and Mabon. It's easy to think in black-and-white, absolute terms: *Summer's over. The sun's gone. Only darkness lies ahead.* Let's pause today and find our balance.

Find a bench in a public place and sit for a while. Be fully present and attentive. Notice the details of what is happening around you; see what has been taken for granted or overlooked. Slow down the turn of the seasons with complete awareness and appreciation of the beauty that surrounds you. Enjoy the flowers and greenery, and smile at people. Delight in summer dresses and shorts. Laugh with the kids playing, still free from school for a few more days. These long moments of attention will slow down time, as if you have slipped between the worlds. Let go of worry and attachment. Release your judgments. Become attuned to the miracle of this moment, and find your balance.

Dallas Jennifer Cobb

August 16

Wednesday

4th ♊

Color of the day: Topaz
Incense of the day: Honeysuckle

Sky-high Splendor

Tiptoe through the tulips this afternoon with Mercury, god of intellect, philosophy, and splendor. Find a windy location and sit quietly as life moves all around you. Envision the winged professor of truth as he moves rapidly near. His azure thighs propel him like a sylph skating through the sky.

Catch hold of his caduceus and fly away with Mercury as he visits the moment of cosmic creation, the evolution of life on earth, the decline of nature, and the collapsing reformation of the universe. Travel with him until at last you return to our own time. Take a moment to thank your winged messenger and then slowly settle back into your body. Listen to the sounds of life all around you. Share your experiences with someone and debate the rationale or philosophy of magic to fully honor Mercury in observance of his rulership today.

Estha McNevin

NOTES:

August 17
Thursday

4th ♊

☽ v/c 9:38 am

☽ → ♋ 12:13 pm

Color of the day: Turquoise
Incense of the day: Apricot

Calling on the Goddess

For many Witches, connecting with the Goddess is an important part of their spiritual practice. No matter how you envision her or what name you use, it is a good idea occasionally to take time for a little chat with our great Mother. This is a good spell to use under a full moon, but really there is no wrong time to call to the Goddess:

> Great Goddess, fair lady of the moon,
>
> Maiden, mother, and crone,
>
> Enchantress, huntress, wise one,
>
> Come to me now and share your wisdom.
>
> Grant me a moment of your grace and peace.
>
> Comfort me with your deep and abiding love,
>
> And know that I love you back with all of my heart.

> Great Goddess, I call to you.
>
> Great Goddess, I call to you.
>
> Great Goddess I call to you.
>
> In perfect love and perfect trust I call.
> Deborah Blake

Notes:

August 18

Friday

4th ♋

Color of the day: Purple
Incense of the day: Cypress

National Parks and Protected Spaces

It's Friday and the weekend is almost here. We're at the height of summer and good times abound. Before you head out this weekend, take a moment to remember our national parks, which so many of us flock to this time of year.

In 1951, the arrowhead became the symbol of the National Park Service. A bison, sequoia trees, mountains, and water are incorporated into this logo.

For this spell, draw an arrowhead. Write on your arrowhead things you love about protected spaces and national parks. Light a green candle and give thanks for all the blessings we receive from spending time in nature. Light the paper from the candle and allow the paper to burn to ashes in a fireproof container. Let the candle burn down. Scatter the ashes the next time you're in an open space or national park.

Najah Lightfoot

August 19

Saturday

4th ♋

☽ v/c 11:17 am
☽ → ♌ 1:55 pm

Color of the day: Black
Incense of the day: Ivy

Cicada Song

Here in the United States, the heat of the summer is upon us, bringing with it the song of the cicada. Jarring to some, melodious to others, the song was music to the ears of the ancients.

Cicadas represent rebirth, resurrection, carefree living, and immortality. They signify extreme good luck. References to the insect are found in Homer's *Iliad*. Sacred to Apollo and considered a delicacy by Aristotle, cicadas appear in ancient Chinese artworks.

Never kill a cicada. However, if you spot a dead one, you can preserve it in a jar with a glycerin packet. Keep it in a cool, dry spot for positive energy. It can also be used on your altar for various healing or prosperity spells.

Emyme

August 20

Sunday

4th ♌

Color of the day: Gold
Incense of the day: Heliotrope

The Magick Box

Create your own "magick box," a treasure trove of goodies and items full of magickal potential.

You'll need a small box—ideally made of natural materials. Decorate it to suit your purposes or preferences with words, sigils, symbols, decorative papers or tape, or whatever inspires you. On the inside of the lid, write: "Magick Box: Take Something/Leave Something." Fill the box with items that could be used for magickal workings: beads, crystals, stones, small figurines, twigs, scraps of fabric, small candles, marbles, miniature tarot cards, or whatever you can find.

When the need for magick seizes you, open the box and say:

Deep into this box I reach.

Answers, now, my fingers seek.

Pull an item—it will probably be exactly what you need! You can use the box for divination, too: ask a question and pull a response. Be sure to keep adding to the contents as well. May your magick box grow ever in power!

Susan Pesznecker

August 21

Monday

4th ♌

☽ v/c 2:30 pm

New Moon 2:30 pm

☽ → ♍ 4:25 pm

Color of the day: Ivory
Incense of the day: Clary sage

Solar Eclipse

Eclipse Inspiration

Today is the new moon. There will also be a solar eclipse today at about 2:30 p.m. Eastern time, when the moon travels between the sun and the earth. In the tarot, the Sun card symbolizes day, logic, exposure, manifestation, and success. The Moon card stands for night, intuition, secrets, dreams, and cycles. An eclipse represents the moon venturing into the sun's domain. It is a time when the inner world takes over the outer.

This is the perfect time for a spell to draw insights from deep within the self's well. For this spell, you will need the Sun and Moon cards from a tarot deck and a fishhook on a thread. Sandwich the hook between the cards, with the Moon card on top, and leave them in the light of the eclipse. Then pull the hook from between the cards, visualizing that it brings messages from your intuition. Write down everything that comes to mind, and choose one idea to act on.

Elizabeth Barrette

August 22

Tuesday

1st ♍

☉ → ♍ 6:20 pm

Color of the day: Scarlet
Incense of the day: Basil

Protection Bundle

Make a protection bundle using a combination of herbs and stones. Here are some plants you may already have on hand: basil, clove, dill, fennel, ivy, lavender, lilac, marigold, mint, oak, parsley, rosemary, or sage. Good stone choices include black tourmaline, clear quartz, garnet, iron, obsidian, tiger's eye, and turquoise.

Place your combination inside a red or white drawstring bag or piece of fabric that you can tie closed with a ribbon. Visualize your goal and charge the bundle with these words:

This talisman shall be a guard,

A symbol to protect and shield,

Bringing safety where I go,

Threats or danger be revealed.

Carry the bundle with you.

Ember Grant

August 23

Wednesday

1st ♍

☽ v/c 4:02 pm

☽ → ♎ 9:05 pm

Color of the day: Brown
Incense of the day: Marjoram

Maintaining our Project Garden

The seeds of projects we planted in the spring have become tall plants (see May 9 and June 25). There are some that may have grown out of control and need a little maintenance, while others may not have taken. There also may be too many projects. Time to use air energy so performing projects can breathe.

If any of your projects are out of control, trim them back. Make them more focused. Trim to only that which directly supports your goals.

Other projects may not be doing so well. These are sickly projects. Or you may have too many projects. These are all weeds. They need to be removed. Put these projects to the side for another time. Air wisdom will help you choose what will perform best to support your goals.

Keep focused on final results. Allow the successful projects to breathe. Check the projects regularly and do what is needed to bring them to fruition.

Boudica

August 24

Thursday

1st ♎

Color of the day: Green
Incense of the day: Carnation

healing Affirmation

We all need healing from time to time, whether it is physical, mental, or spiritual. This is a simple affirmation to help with this task. If you like, you can light a white or blue candle and repeat as many times as feels right:

I am strong and serene.

I am healthy and whole.

I am a child of the goddess,

And I am healing.

                              Deborah Blake

♥ **August 25**

Friday

1st ♎

Color of the day: Rose
Incense of the day: Rose

Domestic Blessings

Friday is ruled by Venus (the Norse Frigg or Freya). Before she was conflated with Aphrodite, the Great Creatrix, the Roman Venus was a more modest domestic goddess. Among her charges were conjugal love and herb gardens, but not wildness or overgrowth in either. In fact, when Medieval painters painted the Virgin Mary, they put her in a house or garden (Venus was safe) because going out into the wilderness was considered dangerous (Aphrodite was scary).

Thank Venus for the love and domesticity in your life. Consider your partner, children, parents, grandparents, and even furry friends. Domesticity can include a clean place to live and the wherewithal to buy food and furniture. Make a list of what you love, then say:

Blessed Venus, thank you for the love that is always present in my life. Please teach me how to cultivate that love so that it and I are always fed.

                              Barbara Ardinger

August 26

Saturday

1st ♎

☽ v/c 1:39 am

☽ → ♏ 4:53 am

Color of the day: Gray
Incense of the day: Magnolia

Back to School Safety Spell

A round this time of year, millions of students go back to school to continue their educational trek toward excellence. The astroweather is perfect today to cast this protection spell for anyone you might know who could use a watchful eye as they make their way back to school. All you need is a white square of paper, a black pen, and an apple.

On the white square of paper, write the name of the person you are casting this spell for three times. Rotate the paper clockwise ninety degrees and write SHALL BE PROTECTED three times over the names. Cut the apple in half horizontally to reveal the star in the center. Place the paper in between the two halves and say:

By the star and the fruit, by the tree and the seed, by the earth and the spirits, (name of student) shall be protected!

Then bury the apple near your front door.

Devín hunter

 August 27

Sunday

1st ♏

Color of the day: Amber
Incense of the day: Eucalyptus

Rooting Your Altar

A fter you set up your altar, you may like to activate it as your magical working place. This is a spell to do that by rooting your altar in its new place.

Light the candles on your altar and some incense. I recommend using equal parts of rose, frankincense, myrrh, and dragon's blood for a loose incense. Ground, center, and align.

Focus first on the flames, and with your breath and awareness, see those flames encircling the altar and igniting magic there. Then bring your attention to the smoke and see and feel it encircling the altar and clearing any unwanted forces. Finally, hold the legs or the base of the altar and focus on perceiving strong and vital vines sprouting and sinking down into the earth beneath your home. You will feel when this is complete. So mote it be.

Gede Parma

August 28

Monday

1st ♏︎

☽ v/c 5:38 am

☽ → ♐︎ 3:48 pm

Color of the day: Silver
Incense of the day: Narcissus

Mercury in Retrograde

Mercury remains in retrograde motion for another week. As the school year has begun for many, this may have an impact on students. Pay close attention to instructions. If in doubt, ask questions: never assume. Be clear in your requests and your answers. This holds true for business and personal communication as well.

You can give a boost to any spell you cast during a Mercury retrograde by including the goddess Freya. This Norse goddess rules over language, networking, and social skills. Conversely, she can disguise and deceive. Best to keep on her good side. You may wish to place a picture or symbol of Freya on your altar during the periods when Mercury is moving retrograde. Say:

Freya, goddess of communication,

May my thoughts and words be understood.

May my understanding be clear and true.

I ask this always and especially during times of retrograde.

Emyme

NOTES:

August 29
Tuesday

1st ♐

2nd Quarter 4:13 am

Color of the day: Red
Incense of the day: Cedar

Stone Solid Protection

Stones have been used for many centuries. Why not use them to protect your own domicile? Grab a decorative dish or tray, some polished river stones, and some paint pens. Choose some of the stones to decorate and write on, using meaningful words and protective symbols. Consecrate the stones with a protective oil. I use patchouli since its smell helps reinforce the earthy protective energies of the stones. Then arrange the stones in your container and place somewhere near the main door. Recharge every six months or whenever you feel it's necessary.

Laurel Reufner

August 30
Wednesday

2nd ♐

Color of the day: Topaz
Incense of the day: Lavender

A Magical Wand

People spend a fortune on fancy wands, but the most magical wand is the one you make yourself.

Select in advance a piece of wood that feels good in your hand. Wood can be apple for magic, willow for love, oak for protection, or whatever you like.

Ground and center before you begin. This is a ritual act.

Carve your name into the wood using a magical alphabet, such as runic or Theban. Add other symbols, such as spirals, pentagrams, or astrological signs.

To embed a crystal in the wand, carve an indentation for it. Sand the carved wand until smooth, then glue crystals or other ornaments in place. Then oil the wood with tung or linseed oil.

Finally, wrap the wand with leather strips for a handgrip. You can let the ends of these strips hang and ornament them with beads or feathers.

Consecrate the completed tool by air, fire, water, and earth. Use it immediately.

Deborah Lipp

August 31
Thursday

2nd ♐

☽ v/c 12:42 am

☽ → ♑ 4:18 am

Color of the day: White
Incense of the day: Mulberry

Unlocking Doors

Visit a secondhand store to procure an old book of noticeable character, and fish out any old keys of yours that you can find at home. Using an X-Acto knife, cut a 2 by 3-inch rectangle out of the center of half the pages in the book. Glue the cut edges in the book together using rubber cement so that they create a hidden compartment. Line this with golden felt. Then place the old keys in your secret box.

Hide this book among your magic books for safekeeping. When you study a new subject, write your accreditation goals on a blue ribbon and tie this to a newfound key, then add it to your secret box of offers and opportunities. May the doors of destiny unlock before you!

Estha McNevin

NOTES:

September

September is the ninth month of the year. Its name is derived from the Latin word *septum*, which means "seventh," as it was the seventh month of the Roman calendar. Its astrological sign is Virgo the maiden (August 23–September 23), a mutable earth sign ruled by Mercury. September is the dreamy golden afternoon of the year. Summer thins away, but September is a treasure chest filled with bounty and color. Apples ripen in the orchards. Purple grapes are harvested, and yellow heads of goldenrod nod along the roadsides. At Mabon, we celebrate the autumn equinox, and the dual nature of life/death. Now we're reminded of the goddess Demeter, and how her period of mourning for her abducted daughter Persephone coincides with nature's decline. To honor Demeter, drape your altar with purple fabric, and upon it place one red apple. Meditate about what you have and what you wish for. Bury the apple as you visualize your wish coming true. By September's end, autumn's flame begins to burn. You can see it in the orange of the maples and in the purple wild asters. Golden September—it's a time to dream, and a time to make those dreams come true.

James Kambos

September 1

Friday

2nd ♑

Color of the day: Purple
Incense of the day: Yarrow

Protecting a Child

You and your child can create bedtime guardians against things that go bump in the night. Place an elemental doll at each of the compass points in your child's room.

In the east, hold your child's hand, facing the doll—a bird or winged fairy—and say:

You are the guardian of the east. Your job is to protect this room from all flying things and all things of air. So be it!

Repeat this in each direction. The doll of the south is a lizard, lion, or tiger. It protects from *all creepy-crawlies and all things of fire.* The doll of the west is a fish, whale, or dolphin and protects from *all dark things, bad dreams, and all things of water.* The doll of the north is a bear, pig, or bull and protects from *all hidden things, anything underground, and all things of earth.*

Return to the east and say:

Now this room is safe. These guardians watch over (your child's name) whether in their quarter or in his/her bed. So be it.

Deborah Lipp

September 2

Saturday

2nd ♑

☽ v/c 12:30 pm
☽ → ♒ 4:06 pm

Color of the day: Blue
Incense of the day: Sandalwood

Open to Learning

For many people, children and adults alike, September is back-to-school month. This is a good time to remind ourselves of the importance of continually learning. After all, without new knowledge, how can we grow and change?

Say this spell to open yourself to learning new things about the world around you and about your own internal landscape. If you like, you can light a yellow candle to signify the power of air, which governs the mind.

I am open to learning,

To knowing and becoming,

To seeing that which will aid me in my journey,

To hearing what is said by those who are wiser.

I will open my eyes, my heart, and my mind.

I am open to learning and to positive growth.

So mote it be.

Deborah Blake

September 3
Sunday

2nd ♒

Color of the day: Yellow
Incense of the day: Hyacinth

Planting Intentions

Autumn is the ideal time to plant bulbs that produce spring flowers. Snowdrops, crocus, daffodils, tulips, and hyacinths all go into the ground this season. There is no immediate reward; they work their magic in secret, underground, all winter. So it's a perfect parallel for making future plans.

For this spell, you will need a bag of flower bulbs—any kind will do—and some plans with a timespan of several months. Begin by meditating. Hold each bulb in your hands and concentrate on what you wish to accomplish. Then plant the bulbs. As you bury each one, say:

Earth, receive these bulbs, like seeds.

Hold them close through cold and doubt.

Swell and grow my thoughts, my needs,

Underground till spring, then sprout.

Keep the card from the bag to remind you how beautiful your flowers—and achievements—will be in spring, as you work through winter.

Elizabeth Barrette

September 4
Monday

2nd ♒

Color of the day: Gray
Incense of the day: Neroli

Labor Day

Give Thanks

This is the end of the working summer. We remember that life is not always about doing our job. It is also a time to remember that we have families and friends. Relax and have a good time.

But remember to give thanks to your special influences that allow you to spend this time with family and friends, be it your gods, the universe, or just your own hard work and efforts. Be grateful for your skills, your health, and the friendship of those around you. The best way to say thanks is to make time for those who are important to us. Remember, they also enable you to succeed by supporting you.

Remember the summer for the pleasures you had with family and good friends. These are the memories that will keep you warm through the colder months to come and make you look forward to next summer.

Boudica

September 5
Tuesday

2nd ♒

☽ v/c 1:15 am

☽ → ♓ 1:28 am

Color of the day: Maroon
Incense of the day: Ginger

New Clothes, New Shoes

It's September. School has started or will start soon. At this time of year, parents and students of all ages acquire new clothes and shoes for the school year. Some buy brand-new items, while others receive items that are new to them. Either way, "new" clothes and shoes will make their way into the lives of many.

Before classes start, take a moment to think of all who made your clothes, the materials from which they are made, and the living things that gave of their being for your clothes and shoes. All things come from the earth, and it is to her that we owe our thanksgiving.

Light a sage bundle. As you pass it over your belongings, say:

Earth Mother, we thank you for all we have received.

Thank you for fulfilling our every need.

Extinguish the sage bundle and enjoy your new clothes!

Najah Lightfoot

September 6
Wednesday

2nd ♓

☽ Full Moon 3:03 am

☽ v/c 4:29 pm

Color of the day: White
Incense of the day: Honeysuckle

Full Moon in Pisces
Intuition Spell

When in convergence with the moon, the power of Pisces is known for producing intense psychic phenomena and sensitivity. We can harness this energy and use it to activate, cleanse, and restore our psychic abilities. To perform this spell, all you need is a bowl of water and moonlight.

Place the bowl of water under the moonlight and allow it to charge for no less than ninety minutes. Draw a pentacle of white fire over the bowl and say:

I call upon the power of the Pisces moon and summon it into this water. May it cleanse and restore what has been dulled. May it empower what is weak, and may it awaken the psychic fires within!

Under the moonlight, wash your third eye, hands, and feet with this water and say:

So must it be.

Devin Hunter

♌ **September 7**

Thursday

3rd ♓

☽ → ♈ 8:01 am

Color of the day: Crimson
Incense of the day: Balsam

Numerological Jewelry

Pythagoras said, "Numbers rule all things." Let us therefore consider the numerological significance of our jewelry. There are many books and websites that give the meanings of numbers. Find out what you're wearing. For example:

Gold = 7 + 6 + 3 + 4 = 20 = 2. The number two signifies balance and partnership. Card II in the major arcana of the tarot (the High Priestess).

Silver = 1 + 9 + 3 + 4 + 5 + 9 = 31 = 4. Four means stability and order, plus all the things (like the sides of a square and seasons) that come in fours. Card IV in the major arcana (the Emperor).

Diamond = 4 + 9 + 1 + 4 + 6 + 5 + 4 = 33. Thirty-three, called the "master builder," focuses on humanitarian issues. Reduced to six, it means spiritual growth and high ideals. Card VI in the major arcana (the Lovers).

We Pagans like to wear precious and semiprecious stones and metals for the energies they carry. Gold is solar and projective, while silver is lunar and receptive. Diamonds are also solar and projective. Use numerology to help you decide what jewelry to wear to add desired energies to your life.

Barbara Ardinger

Notes:

September 8

Friday

3rd ♈

Color of the day: Coral
Incense of the day: Orchid

A Spell to Calm Anger

Has it been one of those days? It started off with your irritating, nosy neighbor. Then you got to work and someone had your parking space, and your boss acted like a jerk all day. If that weren't enough, a certain coworker didn't lift a finger.

Instead of giving everyone dirty looks, try this spell when you get home to calm your anger. First, make a list of everything that made you angry today. Then tear up the paper and put it in a heatproof dish. Over the paper, sprinkle some dried sage and ignite it. As the smoke curls about you, say:

> My spirit is cleansed by this sage.
>
> I hold no grudges or hate.
>
> I hereby release all anger and rage.

Let the sage and paper burn until only ashes are left. When cool, throw them in the trash.

James Kambos

September 9

Saturday

3rd ♈

☽ v/c 11:52 am
☽ → ♉ 12:23 pm

Color of the day: Indigo
Incense of the day: Sage

Herbal Harvest Spell

Herbal magicks can empower your spells, particularly if you harvest and prepare them yourself. For this spell, you'll need gathering tools (a sharp boline or plant shears, a shovel), plant food or organic fertilizer, and pure water.

Identify the living plant or tree you wish to use, making sure it is nontoxic and not imperiled. Using a ritual tool or your finger, cast a magick circle around the plant, asking for protection from earth, air, fire, and water. Ask Gaia for permission to gather the plant:

> Mother Gaia, bringer and sustainer of life, I ask to harvest from this plant for my magickal purposes, taking only what I need. I bring this offering.

Scatter plant food or fertilizer around the plant's base. Wait for a sign giving an answer to your request. Then gather only what you need from the plant, and before leaving, make a second offering of water to the plant. Close the circle, give thanks to the plant's spirit, and depart.

Susan Pesznecker

September 10
Sunday

3rd ♉

☽ v/c 8:54 pm

Color of the day: Gold
Incense of the day: Juniper

Renewing Bath

Recharge your batteries after a long day with a comforting ritual bath. Gather some bubble bath, Epsom or bath salts, a candle, a lighter, and something on which you can play music. Ideally all of the scented items will match—lavender is recommended, but eucalyptus is another good one. So are citrus scents.

Run a nice warm bath full of bubbles, adding in about a half cup of salts to the water. Light the candle and set it on the edge of the tub. Play some music that you find relaxing and uplifting. Turn off the lights, sink into the bubbly warm water, and enjoy your soak, visualizing all of the day's trials, stresses, and tribulations melting away into the water. Emerge renewed and recharged.

Laurel Reufner

September 11
Monday

3rd ♉

☽ → ♊ 3:29 pm

Color of the day: Silver
Incense of the day: Rosemary

Wheel of Global Peace

While on a walk today, gather eight fallen twigs, each about twenty inches long; look for ones that call to you. Using rainbow-dyed cotton twine, bind the twigs into four crossed pairs, balancing all the opposites in the world. Next, affix each crossed pair to another, creating two wheels. Lace the two wheels together, weaving any excess twine between the twigs to tie off each wheel at the center. Weave three feet of braided twine and tie this to hang as a central line.

Finally tie varying lengths of twine tightly onto each twig. Add a cultural charm or item of religious jewelry onto each loose thread to dangle down. It's okay to start with just a few items that you have on hand and add more over the season as a family project. Display this artful mobile above a table, reading nook, or family sofa to evoke peace and human rights within your home.

Estha McNevin

September 12
Tuesday

3rd ♊

Color of the day: Red
Incense of the day: Ylang-ylang

Clearing Nervousness

Find a place out on the land, in the city, or in your home that you feel supported by. To this place, bring some water and a vessel to pour it into. Also bring a jet stone and some red thread.

Ground, center, and align. You may feel like demarcating a space in which to concentrate your work. Pour the water into the vessel and drink it. As you drink the water, perceive a waterfall of cleansing light flowing down through you, from top to bottom. While holding the jet stone and red thread, begin to allow any nervousness you hold to surface, and concentrate it into the thread. When you feel it is firmly in that thread, tie the thread around the stone until the black is almost unnoticeable. Find a place where you can bury the stone and thread, then leave the place without looking back.

Gede Parma

September 13
Wednesday

3rd ♊
4th Quarter 2:25 am
☽ v/c 2:35 pm
☽ → ♋ 6:12 pm

Color of the day: Brown
Incense of the day: Lilac

Banquet for the Gods

An honorary banquet called Epulum Jovis was once held each year on this day in ancient Rome. It's described as a kind of thanksgiving feast. People dined in honor of Minerva, Juno, and Jupiter and decorated with statues of these deities, as though the gods were among them.

Invite the deities of your choice to dinner. The layout need not be extravagant; it's the intent that counts. Be sure to have statues or other representations of the honored guests on the table. Thank them for their gifts. Here's a toast you can use:

For all the gifts you've given me,

I offer something back to thee.

A symbol of my gratitude,

A gift of drink, a gift of food.

After the feast, leave a bit of food and drink outside as an offering. Pour a bit of drink on the ground; bread, fruit, or nuts are good choices for food offerings.

Ember Grant

September 14
Thursday

4th ♋

Color of the day: Green
Incense of the day: Clove

Let Go of Attachment

Kids are back in school and life has shifted. It's time to let go and move on with a "release and reaffirm" ritual. You will need two sheets of paper, a pen, matches, a burning bowl, and your busy mind.

Choose a private spot, preferably outdoors. Sit on the earth to ground, and know that you are supported and protected. Take deep breaths to center yourself, then make two lists: "What I Release" and "What I Reaffirm." Do this quickly, without too much analysis or doubt. Let your deepest self speak. For the first list, you might write:

I release busyness, obligation, impatience, gossip, stress, and worry.

Then on the second sheet:

I reaffirm my center, how spiritual connection feels. I reaffirm self-care, and how necessary it is to everything else that I care about.

Now carefully burn both lists in your burning bowl. Let go of your attachment to "good" and "bad." Release and be at peace.

Dallas Jennifer Cobb

September 15
Friday

4th ♋

☽ v/c 5:23 pm
☽ → ♌ 9:09 pm

Color of the day: Pink
Incense of the day: Thyme

Grasshoppers

The weather was temperate and end-of-summer insects were abundant. I first noticed the grasshopper after I was well on my way, driving, with no place to pull over. It clung to the front passenger window for eight miles. Amazing! Upon reaching my destination, I gently removed it and placed it in the grass. The next day, I discovered a grasshopper clinging to the inside of the screen of my patio door. I knew at that moment that someone, somewhere, was trying to get my attention. Grasshoppers leap forward and bring good luck to any future endeavor. I cherish the messages sent by my little green friends and gladly face whatever comes next.

Happy grasshopper, harbinger of good luck,

I'm grateful for your visit,

A reminder to look to the future.

All is well, all will be well.

All will always be well.

Emyme

September 16

Saturday

4th ♌

Color of the day: Gray
Incense of the day: Patchouli

Lungs of the Earth

The earth is a living, breathing organism. Although humans appear to exist separately from the earth, in truth we do not. We are all intimately connected.

Have you ever noticed how much better you feel when you are in a forest or sitting in a park? Without any effort, your breathing slows, your heart relaxes, and your spirit is renewed as if a spell had been cast.

We owe this goodness to trees. Trees take in carbon dioxide and release oxygen. They inhale and exhale with us. Trees are sacred. They are one of the oldest living species on earth.

Take a moment to be with a tree. Place one hand on your heart and one hand on the tree. Thank the tree for all it gives to us and to our planet.

Najah Lightfoot

September 17

Sunday

4th ♌

☽ v/c 8:55 pm

Color of the day: Orange
Incense of the day: Almond

Snipping the Threads

To break your attachment to someone from the past or someone who is bad for you, cut the threads of attachment.

Wet a pair of sewing scissors in saltwater, saying:

By water and earth, I consecrate this tool of cutting. Cut away attachments!

Pass the scissors through burning sage smoke, saying:

By fire and air, I consecrate this tool of cutting. Cut away attachments!

Then say:

By all powers, I do cut away the threads between (persons's name) and me.

With the scissors, make three cuts beneath the soles of your feet (cutting the aura), saying:

I cut (name) from my feet.
Where I walk, (name) is not.

Repeat the three aura cuts at the following locations, saying the appropriate verse.

Root:

I cut (name) from my root.
At my root, (name) is not.

Navel:

> I cut (name) from my navel.
> In my gut, (name) is not.

Heart:

> I cut (name) from my heart.
> When I love, (name) is not.

Hands:

> I cut (name) from my hands.
> What I touch, (name) is not.

Throat:

> I cut (name) from my throat.
> What I say, (name) is not.

Third eye:

> I cut (name) from my third eye.
> In my imagination, (name) is not.

Crown:

> I cut (name) from my crown.
> In my dreams, (name) is not.

Then say:

> It is done.

Keep the scissors on your altar. Afterward, clean and oil the scissors so the salt doesn't damage them.

Deborah Lipp

 September 18

Monday

4th ♌

☽ → ♍ 12:52 am

Color of the day: Ivory
Incense of the day: Clary sage

To Bless a Magical Pouch

The vessels in which we choose to carry our magical tools and items are sometimes just as important as the items themselves but are tasked with the job of keeping them all secure. This spell can be cast at any time during the day and merely requires your favorite blessing incense and the bag you intend to use.

Light your incense and hold the bag in both hands. Take three deep breaths, and as you do so, feel the energy within the bag grounding along with your own energy. Pass the bag through the incense several times and chant:

> Smoke, smoke, smoke, smoke,
> swirling sacred round and round.
>
> Smoke, smoke, smoke, smoke,
> here new magic shall be found!

Open the bag, take a deep breath, and exhale into it as if to give it life. Put the bag under your pillow for one night before using.

Devin Hunter

September 19
Tuesday

4th ♏

Color of the day: White
Incense of the day: Geranium

Texters Walking in the Streets

It happens every day. We're in our car and we see someone crossing a busy street, their eyes glued to their smartphone. Traffic? What traffic? Or we encounter someone riding a bicycle or skateboard (in the middle of the street!) and texting or catching up on Facebook instead of paying attention. How many near misses have you had with these people? Do they ever see anything that's not on that little screen?

It's time to cast a spell. As tempted as you may be, don't yell out the window of your car. Don't gesticulate at the person hypnotized by their device. Instead, slow down, take a deep breath, and visualize the person becoming aware of the world. Send this invocation gently in their direction:

Smartphone user, look up, look up!

Please stop texting while you walk.

Find a seat where you'll be safer

And enjoy your day of text and talk.

Barbara Ardinger

September 20
Wednesday

4th ♏
☽ v/c 1:30 am
New Moon 1:30 am
☽ → ♎ 6:06 am

Color of the day: Topaz
Incense of the day: Lavender

A New Moon Glamour Spell

This New Moon occurs during the Virgo-Libra cusp, as the sun transitions from Virgo into Libra. Since each of these signs is associated with appearance and refinement, this cusp is known as "the cusp of beauty." Now is the time to perform a glamour spell. You'll need a mister filled with rose water, a silver candle, and a mirror.

Mist yourself lightly with the rose water, then light the candle. Look into the mirror and notice any areas you wish to improve. Look at the candle and say:

From my head to my toes,

A new and glamorous me grows.

As the moon grows, keep working on your goals, such as hair, diet, skin— anything you want. Keep in mind the charm you spoke when you started the spell. When the spell makes the transformation you want, treat yourself to some new fall clothes.

James Kambos

♥ September 21

Thursday

1st ♎

Color of the day: Purple
Incense of the day: Jasmine

UN International Day of Peace –
Rosh hashanah – Islamic New Year

Fierce Love Spell

We are very near to the fall equinox. These times are often revolutionary and provocative. Do you desire a lover? Do you desire to be a fierce lover? Fierce love is a powerful concept and invocation. It is not something to invoke lightly either.

Make an altar with images, symbols, scents, and objects you consider to embody fierce love. A fierce lover is one who is a warrior for truth, who understands that vulnerability is strength and bravery is poetry. Fierce love is consensual, shared, and planted in the wild heart.

Light red and black candles on the altar and move nine times around it. When you are done, be seated before the altar and make a gesture to bare your heart. Hold this gesture for as long as you can. Cry out:

I am a fierce lover and I open to fierce love!

Gede Parma

NOTES:

September 22

Friday

1st ♎

☽ v/c 9:04 am

☽ → ♏ 1:40 pm

☉ → ♎ 4:02 pm

Color of the day: Rose
Incense of the day: Vanilla

Mabon – Fall Equinox

homemade Potpourri

To celebrate the season, make your own fall potpourri to freshen a room for several months. Begin by thinly slicing one apple and one orange and baking them on a cookie sheet lined with parchment paper at 250 degrees Fahrenheit until they're dried—it could take up to six hours (alternately, let them sit for several days in a dry place). Turn them over at least once while baking.

Remove from oven, then dust them with cinnamon and nutmeg (or pumpkin pie spice) and allow them to cool. Place them in a decorative jar or bowl with cinnamon sticks, star anise, cloves, and any other items of your choice. You may be able to find cinnamon-scented pine cones at a craft or hobby store. Here's a celebratory chant to welcome the season:

Longer nights and shorter days,

Feel the sunlight's waning rays.

Welcome autumn, changing leaves,

Hint of winter on the breeze.

Ember Grant

Notes:

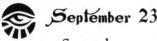

September 23
Saturday

1st ♏

Color of the day: Blue
Incense of the day: Rue

Autumn Leaf Divination

In autumn, leaves fall from trees. If you walk around your yard or a park, you'll find many different types of fallen leaves. Each has its own shape and symbolism. Gather at least half a dozen different ones. For accuracy, include a mix of positive and negative meanings.

There are various methods of divination. One is to float the leaves in a large basin of water and see which reaches the far side first. Another is to blow them with a fan and see which goes farthest. Have a friend throw them from a window and try to catch one. Whichever you get tells you about what the coming season will bring you.

Here are what some common trees symbolize:

    Ash—healing
    Birch—family
    Elder—wisdom
    Hedge apple—bitterness
    Linden—foresight
    Maple—sweetness
    Oak—strength
    Poplar—hope
    Rowan—power
    Willow—sorrow

Elizabeth Barrette

September 24
Sunday

1st ♏
☽ v/c 3:33 am

Color of the day: Amber
Incense of the day: Marigold

Day in Court

Court is all about justice. Sometimes the end result is not what we anticipated, but we cannot expect to get all that we want. We do expect that justice will be done.

My favorite working for any court case is simple. You will need a purple candle dressed with High John oil and the Justice card from a tarot deck. I like seven-day candles for a long-term effect from the working. The more you put in, the more you get out. The intent for this working is that justice be on your side. Light the candle and use the Justice card to focus your intent.

The gods to call upon are varied. Our American Lady Justice is based on the Roman goddess Iustitia. We also have Maat from the Egyptian pantheon. The Greek goddess Themis is divine order, and Dike, her daughter, carries the scales of balance. Astraea is also associated with innocence and justice. Look to these deities for a favorable outcome.

Boudica

September 25

Monday

1st ♏

☽ → ♐ 12:01 am

Color of the day: Lavender
Incense of the day: Lily

harvesting happiness

By the end of September, the harvest is in full force in most places. Corn and squash and apples are wonderful symbols of the season, but don't forget to do magical work to harvest the less tangible things that you planted the seeds for earlier in the year. If your crop needs a little boost, this spell is a good way to nourish it.

If you can, say this outside with your feet on the land. But if you can't, just take a moment to open yourself to the harvest energy all around. If you have an altar, decorate it with seasonal vegetables. Say:

I planted my seeds for happiness and joy,

Success and prosperity, healing and love.

And now I wish to harvest my bounty

With the blessings of the gods above.

So mote it be.

Visualize all those things you wish to harvest in your life.

Deborah Blake

September 26

Tuesday

1st ♐

Color of the day: Scarlet
Incense of the day: Cinnamon

Your Deepest Desires

We work, worry, pay bills, and make appointments. When we're busy, it's usually our most intimate undertakings that get pushed aside—relationships neglected, creativity abandoned, self-care lost.

Today, take care of the mundane details of your life *and* make space for dreamtime. Take your lunch to a quiet spot, leaving the work crew or your family behind. If you work outside the home, use your commute time to get in touch with your deepest desires. Ask yourself:

What is my heart's desire?

Listen carefully to what arises. Ask:

Where will I plant these seeds?

Identify a half-hour slot in your day when you could regularly invest in your dreams. When the seed is planted, our deepest desires grow. Next year you could have a completed manuscript, written in half-hour increments at lunch, or a healing daily meditation practice, undertaken completely on public transit. Today, seed your deepest desires.

Dallas Jennifer Cobb

🔥 September 27
Wednesday

1st ♐

☽ v/c 7:08 am

☽ → ♑ 12:24 pm

2nd Quarter 10:54 pm

Color of the day: Yellow
Incense of the day: Bay laurel

Cleansing, Charging, and Blessing a Stone or Crystal

When acquiring a new stone or crystal, it will benefit from being magickally prepared before use.

Cleanse your stone with the four elements: bury it in salt or soil, allow it to sit in the open breeze, charge it in direct sunlight, and immerse it in pure water, allowing twenty-four hours (longer if possible) for each step.

Charge your stone by leaving it on your altar for twenty-four hours, accompanied by your most important magickal tools and items during this process. If the stone will be used for lunar magicks, it should charge through a full lunar cycle, including time sitting in the full moon's light.

To bless your stone, rise at dawn. Lift it toward the rising sun (east) and then to the south, west, and north, saying:

Powers of the universe, may this stone be blessed to purpose, and may I use it with knowledge and respect.

Keep the stone close to you for the next nine days.

Susan Pesznecker

NOTES:

September 28

Thursday

2nd ♑

Color of the day: Turquoise
Incense of the day: Carnation

Willful Aim

Practice your powers of willful living with a bit of short-term goal setting. To evoke meticulously planned success, acquire eight small sheets of gold leaf–specked rice paper from an origami or stationery supply store. Draw a vivid blue arrow on each one using a nontoxic marker. Flip the sheets over and on the back of each, draw a circle with a dot in the middle. Within this circle, write a goal that you are currently striving to achieve.

Fold each small sheet into a paper arrow or airplane. Launch these darts into the back of your kitchen cupboards and pantry shelves. As they hide in the recesses of your family larder, they will generate luck and manifestation around all of the foods that you eat. This will energetically fuel your success and remind you with every meal why the liberty of a willful life is worth striving a little bit harder for.

Estha McNevin

September 29

Friday

2nd ♑
☽ v/c 8:14 pm

Color of the day: Coral
Incense of the day: Rose

Keepers of the Alphabet

A sizable garden orb-weaving spider appeared at my bedroom window early one morning. The web was large, covering almost the entire window, and thankfully it was on the outside of the glass pane. This allowed me to get quite close. Every morning for a week or so, the spider was there. Sometimes a future meal lay wrapped and suspended in the web. Before the sun rose all the way, the spider would be gone. One day I waited and watched to see where the spider went. It grabbed the meal, slowly descended the web, and crawled under a tab of siding.

A hard rain destroyed the web one night, and the spider never reappeared. It was simply fascinating to watch and such an inspiration to me. Spiders are the keepers of the alphabet, and being a writer, I took this to mean I'd better stop procrastinating and get working on several upcoming projects.

Teotihuacan and Arachne,

Spider women of all legends,

Spinners, weavers, keepers of the alphabet,

Your beauty and perseverance

Inspire us in all things domestic and literate.

ἔmyme

NOTES:

  September 30

Saturday

2nd ♑

☽ → ♒ 12:40 am

Color of the day: Black
Incense of the day: Magnolia

Yom Kippur

Day of Forgiveness

Forgiveness is a tricky thing, and it's usually far easier to forgive others than to forgive ourselves. Today is Yom Kippur within the Jewish tradition, a day of atonement for the sins of the year past. Why not perform a simple ritual of forgiveness for yourself today?

Light a white candle and gather a pad of paper, a favored writing implement, and a bar of chocolate. Get comfy and light the candle. On the paper, list the things that you need to work toward forgiveness for. As you write each item, take a moment to dwell on it and remind yourself of why you deserve to be forgiven. When you're done, burn the list in a fireproof bowl, then sit back and enjoy the chocolate as you contemplate life without those burdens. Repeat as often as necessary.

Laurel Reufner

October

October is a busy month. Originally the eighth month of the year (*octo* being eight) in the Roman calendar, it was set back to the tenth month around 700 BCE, when King Numa Pompilius revised the calendar and added January and February.

The ancient Egyptians celebrate the Festival of Het-Hert, or Hathor, on October 4th. The Romans celebrate Meditrinalia on October 11th, tasting the new wine for the first time and honoring Jupiter as god of the wine. And the Celts close out their year at Samhain on October 31st.

In October, we are most aware of the shortening of the days, the cooling weather, the changing colors of the trees and the falling of the leaves, glowing fires, orange pumpkins, and warm scarves and mittens.

The last of the harvest festivals arrives at Halloween. The veil thins, and we feel the presence of our ancestors and those we cherish who have passed over. We set a place at the table for them and celebrate with them the passing of another season and the closing of another year.

The larders are full against the coming winter months. The last mornings of October bring the killing frosts, and we wait prepared for the change in season yet to come.

Boudica

October 1

Sunday

2nd ≈≈

Color of the day: Orange
Incense of the day: Juniper

Magical Sticky Notes

What on earth would we do without sticky notes? The Post-it Note was invented by accident in 1968 by a chemist named Spencer Silver. He was looking for a strong adhesive, but what he found was a low-tack adhesive that would stick to things but could be easily unstuck and moved. Today, sticky notes come in a multitude of sizes, shapes, and colors.

If you haven't already done so, add sticky notes to your magical repertoire. Try this. At your next ritual, instead of putting actual things (figures of deities, elemental tools, etc.) on your altar, buy large sticky notes in appropriate colors. Draw gods and goddesses, elemental beings, astrological symbols, etc., on them and stick them to your altar(s). Invoke the powers drawn and named on the sticky notes. Move the sticky notes when necessary. Just don't try to substitute little pieces of paper for cakes and ale.

Barbara Ardinger

October 2

Monday

2nd ≈≈

☽ v/c 7:13 am

☽ → ♓ 10:26 am

Color of the day: White
Incense of the day: Narcissus

Destroy a Curse Spell

If you feel you're having more than just a run of bad luck, try this spell. Even if you think you know who has cursed you, don't mention the person's name as you cast this spell. First, gather seven twigs and tie them together with black ribbon. Start a fire in a heatproof dish or fireplace. Hold the bundle of twigs before the fire and repeat seven times:

Curse, be burned.

Curse, be returned.

Curse, die a natural death.

Curse, die with this fire's last breath!

After the last chant, snap the bundle in two and toss it into the flames. The curse is destroyed when the last ember stops glowing. However, let the ashes sit undisturbed for seven days. Then gather them and toss them randomly outside. Don't keep them or use them for other spells.

James Kambos

October 3

Tuesday

2nd ♓

Color of the day: Red
Incense of the day: Bayberry

Business Success

Business is what you do in the working world. Whether you own the business or you work for the owners, success is measured by how well you do at your job. Raises, bonuses, promotions, and perks are awarded based on job performance. You are the person controlling what you do at your job. Be a conscientious worker. Be prompt and attentive to the needs of the business. This will win you the extras you want. But if you are not noticed, it may seem like it is a wasted effort.

Drawing and attracting spells are easy. Be sure you are doing what you want to be seen. Spread attraction powders around your desk or keep sweets on your desk at work to attract attention. Use Better Business oil to keep and hold the attention of the people you want to impress. Keep yourself out front and working. You will be noticed and your efforts will be rewarded.

Boudica

 October 4

Wednesday

2nd ♓

☽ v/c 3:19 am

☽ → ♈ 4:40 pm

Color of the day: Topaz
Incense of the day: Lilac

Animal Blessing

Today is the feast day of Saint Francis of Assisi, who was well known for his love of nature and animals. Statues of Saint Francis adorn many gardens, and he is celebrated for his embrace of a simple life. On this day, many people perform pet blessings. You can perform one yourself today, or you can bless animals of the wild—or both.

Decorate your altar with statues and images of animals. Give your animal companions special attention today, perhaps a treat or new toy. Say:

Creatures of the world be blessed,

Scaled, shelled, feathered, furred;

In water, fields, caves, and nests,

I celebrate them with these words.

Ember Grant

October 5

Thursday

2nd ♈

Full Moon 2:40 pm

Color of the day: Green
Incense of the day: Myrrh

Sukkot begins

honor the Moon with Yoga

Oh, the myriad names each full moon has! There is not enough space here to write them all. No matter the name of a full moon, it may be honored with a sequence of yoga poses called Chandra Namaskar. This full moon salutation is a quieting series of poses honoring and cultivating the soothing lunar energy. Our internal wisdom, creativity, balance, and intuition are encouraged to surface. Happily, this series is among the least challenging and can be found on the Internet and in books. I urge you to honor the moon with yoga.

Goddess Diana, our Lady of the Moon,

We draw down your power.

Bless us in this full moon salutation.

Emyme

October 6

Friday

3rd ♈

☽ v/c 6:38 pm

☽ → ♉ 7:56 pm

Color of the day: Rose
Incense of the day: Violet

Meet Steel with a Penny

An old superstition says that giving a knife (or any kind of "sharp") is bad luck. Why? Well, because a sharp knife is potentially dangerous. But even more because knives are used to sever or separate things, whether those things be ropes or relationships. People have traditionally avoided exchanging or gifting sharps for fear of damaging the human cords between them.

Fortunately, there's a workaround. If you give or exchange a knife, athame, boline, sword, or other sharp with another person, tape a shiny penny to the item. The recipient can then remove the penny and hand it back to you, effectively "paying the price" for the item and undoing the potentially negative effects.

Copper is a strong conductor of magickal energy and is thus often used in creating wands. It's also associated with love and friendship. Carry a penny in your magickal gear and you'll always be ready to deal with steel.

Susan Pesznecker

October 7
Saturday

3rd ♉

Color of the day: Blue
Incense of the day: Sage

Weekend Wishes

We all look forward to the weekend and getting in a little fun and relaxation. But it can be hard to let go after a long, tough week. Here is a simple prayer to the elements and the gods to help you make the most of your downtime. Light a white candle if you want and say this with enthusiasm:

Fire, water, earth, and air,

God and Goddess, spirits fair,

I greet you now in joy and peace,

My work and labors I release.

Free of stress and free of strife,

I'm ready to partake of life!

Deborah Blake

ꞌOctober 8

Sunday

3rd ♉

☽ v/c 9:45 am

☽ → ♊ 9:44 pm

Color of the day: Gold

Incense of the day: Eucalyptus

Go Back the Way You Came!

Here's a simple spell that will protect your home from attack, negative energy, or any unwanted intrusion, physical or astral.

For this spell, you will need:

- 4 small mirrors
- Saltwater
- Incense and burner
- A wand or an athame
- Tape or glue
- A compass

Anoint the mirrors with saltwater, saying:

By water and earth, you shall reflect all harm away from here.

Anoint the mirrors in incense smoke, saying:

By fire and air, you shall reflect all harm away from here.

Send power into the mirrors with your wand or athame, concentrating on driving away harm. See whatever comes into the mirrors bouncing off them, reflected back the way it came.

Tape or glue each mirror so that the reflecting side is against the wall, facing the outside, on an unobtrusive spot on the wall near the floor, at the exact point of north, east, south, and west in your home, using your compass.

Then stand in the center of your home and say:

All harm is reflected away from here. So be it!

Deborah Lipp

Notes:

October 9

Monday

3rd ♊

Color of the day: Lavender
Incense of the day: Clary sage

Columbus Day ~
Indigenous Peoples' Day

Sail Away

Traditionally this day is celebrated as Columbus Day. However, in recent times, indigenous people have become increasingly disenchanted with this designation celebrating the voyage of Columbus.

With respect to the highly charged emotions surrounding this day, we can use the power of the waning moon to sail away to new horizons, letting go of things that no longer serve us.

For this spell, you will need:

- A four-inch blue candle in a holder

- A small dish filled with water

- Blue glitter

- Eight of Cups tarot card

Place the candle and holder in the dish filled with water. Sprinkle blue glitter over your candle and the water. Place the Eight of Cups tarot card behind the candle.

Quiet your mind, light the candle, and concentrate on the tarot card. Visualize yourself sailing away. As the flame burns down, feel the relief of heading toward a new beginning.

Najah Lightfoot

NOTES:

October 10

Tuesday

3rd ♊

☽ v/c 6:25 pm

☽ → ♋ 11:38 pm

Color of the day: Scarlet
Incense of the day: Cinnamon

Protection from Anger

Banish extreme anger from yourself or others by creating a bind rune that you carry with you. You'll need a small piece of good-quality paper and a black marker to create the rune. Do so by the light of a blue candle.

To make the bind rune, draw a horizontal line about two inches long. In the middle, cross it with a vertical line half that length. Turn each end of the horizontal line into the rune Algiz, which looks like a pitchfork (Y). Starting at the bottom of the vertical line on the right-hand side, draw the rune Uruz, which looks a bit like a tilted n (ᚢ). On the left-hand side, draw Uruz reversed, so that the whole thing looks a bit like a three-pronged fork. Repeat at the top of the vertical line, with the rune now also being upside down.

Fold up the paper and carry it on you.

Laurel Reufner

October 11

Wednesday

3rd ♋

Color of the day: Yellow
Incense of the day: Marjoram

Sukkot ends

Incantation to Kali Ma

As seasons change and wild winds whip the cold toward us, invoke the Great Mother Kali Ma with an incantation. We chant the names of her four arms, which represent the four elements (earth, water, fire, wind—La, Va, Ra, Ya) and the complete cycle of creation and destruction. And we call her name: Kali, from the Sanskrit *kal*, meaning "time." Her right hands are held in the mudras that represent "fear not" and offering. Her left hands hold a bloody sword and a severed head, representing the destruction of ignorance and the dawning of knowledge. Chant to invoke Kali in all of her ferocity and tenderness:

> *La, Va, Ra, Ya...Kali Ma*
>
> *La, Va, Ra, Ya...Kali Ma*
>
> *La, Va, Ra, Ya...Kali Ma*

As you chant, know that you are intimately engaged in the eternal cycle of birth, life, death, and compost—creation and destruction. Just like Kali Ma.

Dallas Jennifer Cobb

October 12

Thursday

3rd ♋

4th Quarter 8:25 am

Color of the day: Turquoise
Incense of the day: Balsam

Watchful Nazar Eyes

Provide a layer of protection to your home using the nazar eye symbol, a circle with an iris and pupil shaded in the center. Gather up all your blue crayons. Encourage your roommates and family members to participate in drawing this symbol on all of your windows and mirrors and every glass surface found in the home. Consider gifting a small prize to the person who draws the most.

This is a fun way to decorate for the Hallows season and enlists everyone's mental focus to keep the home protected. This spell is a real hit with kids of all ages. It reminds us that our good attitude, coupled with the watchful eyes of our helpful companions, can inspire us to maintain our own personal safety and self-protection.

Leave the blue crayon on as long as necessary, or cleanse and redraw seasonally. Remove the crayon easily with a hot, soapy washcloth when you feel the magick is complete.

Estha McNevin

October 13

Friday

4th ♋

☽ v/c 12:00 am

☽ → ♌ 2:41 am

Color of the day: Pink
Incense of the day: Cypress

Fairy Love Spell

Love is a positive addition to anyone's life. There are many types of love, from familial to romantic to deep friendship. Although love spells most often focus on romantic love, they can be tuned to other types as well. This one concentrates on platonic feelings.

Fairies are little spirits who are drawn to nature and to positive emotions. They're also partial to offerings of honey or butter, which they can't easily get by themselves. For this spell, you'll need a hanging fairy ornament, preferably one with a shiny bell on it, and an offering. Hang the ornament in your window and set the offering outdoors on a plate. Then say:

Fairies, watch the world as you fly.

Bring me friends to love, by and by.

When you meet new people, watch for a spark or glow to indicate the ones most compatible with you.

Elizabeth Barrette

October 14

Saturday

4th ♌

Color of the day: Black
Incense of the day: Pine

Milk and honey Bath

There are so many avenues for preventive healthcare. Magic and spellcraft are one option. If you feel that symptoms of sickness are beginning to emerge, here is a bath spell to help you relax and open to healing and vital strength.

Draw a warm bath. Next to the bath, place a bowl of milk and a bowl of honey. If the milk and honey are raw, organic, and local, all the better. Immerse yourself in the bath. Ground, center, and align. Pour the milk into the bath and focus on nourishment and strength from the land rising into the bath. Take the honey and pour it in while concentrating on the sweetness of wellness. Here you may choose to verbally invoke a healing spirit or deity you know to help you with your magic. Relax in the bath as long as it is warm.

Gede Parma

October 15

Sunday

4th ♌

☽ v/c 1:28 am

☽ → ♍ 7:19 am

Color of the day: Yellow
Incense of the day: Frankincense

Appease a Spirit Spell

If you think your home has a spirit in residence, perform this spell. Begin at dusk. On a table near a window or an exterior door, place two taper candles—one white, one black. Between the candles, set a glass of red wine. On a plate, put an apple and a slice of bread, and set the plate next to the wine. Light the candles. In a gentle voice, say this charm:

Spirit, I feel your presence day and night.

Is it you who turns on the lights?

Is it you who makes the pictures fall?

Is it you who knocks on the wall?

For you, I've prepared this special feast.

If you choose to stay, please stay in peace.

If the flames spark, the spirit is near. Let the candles burn awhile. The next day, pour the wine outside and crumble the bread on the ground. Place the apple outside and let it rot.

James Kambos

October 16

Monday

4th ♍

Color of the day: Silver
Incense of the day: Neroli

Dictionary Day

In the past, almost every household, and certainly every classroom, had a dictionary. We have Noah Webster, whose birthday we celebrate today, to thank for that. But Webster was so much more than just the creator of the dictionary. He was instrumental in forming an original and improved system of learning, most of which is still in use. Spellcheck may help us with the letters of words, but a dictionary helps with the meanings.

I am happy to say that my library still houses one of those ubiquitous oversized red books. Should you have a dictionary in your personal library (and I hope you do), take some time today to become reacquainted with it.

Words have power.

Every book holds the magick of words.

A dictionary is the key, the map,

To better understanding of our world of letters.

Let us never take that for granted.

Emyme

 October 17

Tuesday

4th ♍

☽ v/c 7:27 am
☽ → ♎ 1:35 pm

Color of the day: White
Incense of the day: Cedar

Confidence Spell

Need a boost of confidence? Nervous about a social event? Try this spell to boost your best qualities and help you get some attention.

First, look in the mirror. Talk to yourself. Say only positive things—give yourself compliments and remind yourself of your best qualities. Let those characteristics shine. Visualize yourself in the setting, receiving the results you desire. Imagine the best possible outcome.

Light a yellow or white candle and charge a piece of jewelry with these words:

Let my best shine through.

I'm confident and sure.

I'm glowing with a light

That no one can ignore.

Allow the candle to burn out. Wear the jewelry and let it remind you of your true beauty and confidence.

Ember Grant

October 18
Wednesday

4♄ ♎

Color of the day: Brown
Incense of the day: Bay laurel

Pinky Promise

How does it happen that we get too busy to keep in touch with our friends? Even though Facebook and other social media are handy, it's that personal, face-to-face friendship that we need to maintain. If you have a friendship or relationship that you want to cherish forever, even though you and/or your friend may someday move on to new homes or new parts of your lives, you can make a pinky promise now and hold it in your memory.

Go with your friend to a place that's special to the two of you, preferably one that's private and quiet. Talk about how valuable your friendship is. Then speak this declaration (or make up your own words):

Even when we're far apart, I will always cherish our friendship.

To seal your promise, link the pinky fingers of your projective hands (right if you're right-handed) and seal the link by shaking but not breaking the pinky link three times. Then hug your friend. Keep your pinky promise by keeping in touch.

Barbara Ardinger

October 19
Thursday

4♄ ♎

☽ v/c 3:12 pm
New Moon 3:12 pm
☽ → ♏ 9:41 pm

Color of the day: Purple
Incense of the day: Nutmeg

Uranus Opposition Spell

The New Moon at opposition with Uranus means that today is the perfect time to break stale cycles and patterns and prepare for the new and unexpected. If you have been feeling overwhelmed lately, chances are Uranus is pulling on your strings and it is time to call change into your life.

Take a deep breath and spend a few moments thinking about all the things that have you feeling down or overwhelmed. Write it all down on a piece of white paper, then draw a giant circle counterclockwise around what you wrote. Say:

Serpent rise and shed thy skin.

Uranus opposed, let magic begin.

Changing life and turning tide,

Let thy will be far and wide!

Burn the paper safely. Mix the ashes with olive oil, then rub the mixture on your belly. Take a shower, rinse off, and visualize yourself renewed.

Devin Hunter

October 20

Friday

1st ♏

Color of the day: Coral
Incense of the day: Orchid

Sacred Soup

Cook soup in sacred space to share with those you love and fill your home and family with blessings.

Assemble the ingredients of your soup ahead of time. Divide the ingredients into four groups. Potential ingredients and their elements are:

Air: Beans, endive, sage, lemongrass, mace, marjoram, chicory

Fire: Peppers, almost anything hot and spicy, carrots, onion, rosemary

Water: Water, broth

Earth: Salt, barley, corn, potatoes, oats, turnips, beets

With an athame, cast a circle around your kitchen, saying:

In this sacred space
Only good may enter.
All that is cooked here is blessed.
So be it.

Point your athame at each group of ingredients in order, saying:

I consecrate these things of (air/fire/water/earth) to bless and balance this soup with (intelligence/passion/love/abundance).

So be it.

When you have finished cooking, close the circle, saying:

The circle is now ended. The goodness remains. Blessed be.

Leave the first portion outdoors as an offering of thanks for the blessings to be received.

Deborah Lipp

NOTES:

October 21

Saturday

1st ♏

Color of the day: Indigo
Incense of the day: Patchouli

Magical Elixir

As the weather changes, it is common to get sick—a sore throat, cold, or flu. Now is a good time to make a natural remedy that boosts the immune system, reduces liver stress, and fights infection, fatigue, and candida. Make a big jar, and drink one ounce a day throughout the cold and flu season.

You will need the following:

- ¼ cup chopped garlic
- ¼ cup diced onion
- 1 whole habanero pepper
- ¼ cup grated fresh ginger
- 2 tablespoons grated horseradish
- 2 tablespoons turmeric
- 32-ounce bottle organic apple cider vinegar
- 1 large Mason jar

Prep the veggies and fill the Mason jar about ⅔ full of them, then add in the spices on top. Pour in the apple cider vinegar, filling to the top. Close the jar and shake. Keep in a cool, dry place and let ferment, shaking well frequently. After two weeks, strain the mixture through cheesecloth. Keep the liquid in the jar in the fridge, and consume an ounce each day, as needed. A magical elixir!

Dallas Jennifer Cobb

NOTES:

October 22
Sunday

1st ♏

☽ v/c 7:35 am

☽ → ♐ 7:57 am

Color of the day: Amber
Incense of the day: Marigold

hexenspiegel

A hexenspiegel (HEX-un-spee-gull) is a small mirror used as a protective charm to reflect away negative magicks, the evil eye, or other bad omens or intentions, as well as return the negative energy to the sender. Its basis is in German folk magick: translated, it means "witch's mirror." Hexenspiegels may be suspended from cords, fastened to walls, or, in the case of small ones, worn as jewelry.

To make your own hexenspiegel, use a plain mirror or use craft glue to adhere small stones, crystals, beads, or other items of choice to the mirror's edges. Charge the mirror by sprinkling it with salt, passing it through the heat and smoke of a candle, and dabbing it with pure water. Place the hexenspiegel where it will carry out your intention, saying:

Mirror, mirror, on the wall, answer my protective call. Turn away the magick black, with all your pow'r, please send it BACK!

Susan Pesznecker

October 23
Monday

1st ♐

☉ → ♏ 1:27 am

Color of the day: Ivory
Incense of the day: Lily

Prosperity Pumpkin

In this week leading up to Halloween (Samhain), pumpkins seem to be everywhere. Here is some simple prosperity magic you can do with pumpkin seeds, whether they are picked up from the store or scooped out of your own jack-o'-lantern. Use the seeds that are still in the shell (roasted, if at home), since you are symbolically releasing the potential that is held within. Seeds are a nutritional powerhouse because much of the plant's future energy is waiting inside them.

Place some pumpkin seeds in a small bowl and put them on your altar or do this outside under the moon. Light a green or orange candle. Eat a seed after each sentence.

Prosperity is mine.

Success is mine.

Abundance is mine.

Multiplying like the seeds of the pumpkin.

Growing like the leaves and vines.

Releasing potential into my life.

Prosperity, success, and abundance are mine.

So mote it be.

Deborah Blake

NOTES:

October 24
Tuesday

1st ♐

☽ v/c 12:44 pm

☽ → ℣ 8:12 pm

Color of the day: Maroon
Incense of the day: Ginger

Algiz Spell

The Nordic rune Algiz (ᛉ), a trident-shaped rune, is a warding and protective sign. It is also related to the plant world, as it may refer to elk sedge, which in the Anglo-Saxon Rune poem suggests that it is a plant that knows how to defend against intrusion. The Algiz rune can be drawn magically in the air to set a boundary or ward.

Ground and center; deepen into your magical state of mind. Begin in the east with the rising sun and begin to trace Algiz in the air while making the sound *zzz* and beholding the rune shining in flame or light. Move in a direction you find affirming of the creation of these wards and face the other directions to make a full circle. Do not forget to inscribe the rune above and below you as well. Earth the power.

Gede Parma

October 25
Wednesday

1st ℣

Color of the day: Yellow
Incense of the day: Lavender

Harvesting Your Project Garden

Hopefully all the projects you planted are complete (see May 9, June 25, and August 23). Goals you set for yourself in the spring are now matured. If you have followed through and worked your projects faithfully, you will have reached your goals. Congratulations!

Sometimes, though, you may not get exactly what you wanted. Maybe you got close to your goal, or maybe you forgot something. This should not deter you.

Take a break, assess the projects, and figure out why one was a success and another did not reach your goal. Remember, there is no failure. This is a learning process. You need to see what needs to be changed to make this "growing" spell work. Maybe better planning, maybe better tools. Or maybe the plan was not for you, and you need to review the entire project.

This process does work. It may just require some practice. Magic is a practice, and you can repeat this process as necessary.

Boudica

October 26

Thursday

1st ♑

Color of the day: Crimson
Incense of the day: Apricot

Mincemeat Day

Today is Mincemeat Day. Originally this dish consisted of chopped meat, dried fruit, and copious spices. It used up shreds of meat and it preserved food. Over time, the amount of meat and suet decreased, so modern "mincemeat" may contain none at all, only fruits and other ingredients.

Celebrate this holiday by eating mincemeat, whether you buy a mince pie or make your own from scratch. If you can, choose one with actual meat. This is a way of honoring our ancestors and their ingenuity, which is what makes mincemeat pie traditional at major holidays such as Thanksgiving and Christmas or Yule. Before you cut the pie, take time to bless it:

Scraps of meat and fat and fruit,

Frugal dish that's made to suit.

From the past to future flow

Memories that touch and go

Through the sweet that we now see.

So eat up, and blessed be!

Elizabeth Barrette

October 27

Friday

1st ♑

☽ v/c 1:22 am

☽ → ♒ 8:59 am

2nd Quarter 6:22 pm

Color of the day: Purple
Incense of the day: Mint

As Fast as You Can

Not all of our autumnal urges are beneficial, but triggering imagined predatory fears, and learning to face them down while we exercise, is one therapeutically spooky way to teach our mind, body, and spirit how to thrive by working together uniformly, helping us to achieve our goals with good habits.

Bask in the light of the late afternoon along your favorite sunny walking trail. Confront your shadow self with conversations of gossip, fault, and failure. Then stop suddenly and run at your fastest speed toward the sun until you are nearly winded. Don't look back. Stop just as suddenly and meditate quietly in the glow of the sunset. Feel your heart racing the darkness, sensing your heartbeat as you exercise awareness in the moment. Express gratitude for each one of your skills and abilities. Recite the following affirmation, as needed:

*Life, light, and spark, illuminate
the dark.*

Estha McNevin

October 28

Saturday

2nd ≈

Color of the day: Gray
Incense of the day: Ivy

Pineapple Plant Protection

Natives to the West Indies used to place pineapple plants in a protective living fence around their villages. Those leaves can be rather sharp, so they serve as a great natural barrier for predators. It's very easy to obtain a start for your own plant—you simply need to buy a ripe pineapple plant at the grocery store. Make sure it still has the leaves attached.

Simply hack the leaves or crown off the top of the pineapple plant, removing any fruit that may still be attached to the base of the leaves. Stick toothpicks around the outside edge of the pineapple crown, near the base, and place in a small glass of water until it takes root. (The toothpicks keep the greenery from dropping all the way down into the glass, where it will sit and rot.) After you have little roots started, simply plant the pineapple crown in a pot and leave in a sunny location. I'd recommend using a yellow or gold pot to up the protective factor. You'll also need some potting soil, some gravel for drainage, and perhaps a suitable protective gemstone—maybe hematite.

Laurel Reufner

October 29

Sunday

2nd ≈

☽ v/c 12:22 pm
☽ → ♓ 7:46 pm

Color of the day: Gold
Incense of the day: Heliotrope

Lost-in-the-Dark Bells

In some English villages, there are stories and legends (some true) that tell of people who were lost in the dark or fog and were steered away from falling off a cliff or ravine by the sound of church bells. To this day, bells are rung in honor of those people (who usually donated money, in gratitude, to the church). Today is one of those days.

Consider a time in your life when you were helped or guided to safety. Ring your own bells tonight—maybe someone will hear. If you don't have a bell, make sound another way—with music, perhaps. Use this chant and visualize helping someone else or receiving guidance with a situation in which you feel lost:

Lost, then found,

By the sound.

Guide me home

When I roam.

Hear the tone—

I'm not alone.

Ember Grant

October 30

Monday

2nd ♓

Color of the day: Lavender
Incense of the day: Rosemary

Spell to Part the Veil

During this time of year, the veil becomes its thinnest and the walls between the worlds come tumbling down. We can feel these changes and shifts and can harness the energies of the moment to fully part the veil and communicate with those on the other side.

Write the names of those you would like to contact on a piece of paper and go to the nearest graveyard. (Ideally, you would visit the graveyard where the people are buried, but any graveyard will do.) Spend some time walking through the gravestones and make your way to the back part of the property. There, read aloud the names of the dead you wish to communicate with and ask the spirits to aid you in this. As you make your way back to the front, clear off debris from nearby gravestones and thank the spirits in advance for their help.

Devin hunter

 October 31

Tuesday

2nd ♓
☽ v/c 5:08 pm

Color of the day: Black
Incense of the day: Basil

Samhain – halloween

Supper for the Dead

Winds blow, trees creak. Leaves rustle, children giggle. Lighted pumpkins decorate doorsteps and you swear you can hear whispers in the night. It is the time of Samhain and Halloween. Honor the thinning veil and those long past by setting a place for your dearly departed loved ones.

You will need:

+ A black tablecloth
+ Marigolds
+ A vase filled with water
+ A place setting
+ A skull candle
+ Mementos of your loved ones

Cover your table space with the black tablecloth. Place the marigolds in the vase and set on the table. Lay out the place setting. Place the skull candle above the place setting. Add your mementos.

On Samhain night, light the skull candle. Take a moment to be with your loved ones across the veil.
Say:

Your presence is welcome here.

If you choose, please draw near.

Out of sight but never gone,

We welcome you here all night long.

Najah Lightfoot

NOTES:

November

At November's commencement, the veil between the worlds is thin, and spirits linger close to the realm of the living. The Mayan Day of the Dead celebration continues until the seventh day of the month, when deceased loved ones and other spirits are bid farewell with a banquet. As the month progresses, the days get shorter and colder, and we take refuge in home, family, cozy blankets and clothes, candles, and the hearth. It's a time to rest after the hard work of the year's literal or metaphorical harvest, and to honor and enjoy the fruits of our labor. Midmonth, the Leonid meteor shower makes an appearance. Named after the constellation of Leo, from which they appear to emanate, the Leonid meteors herald the smoldering end of the sun's stay in Scorpio as well as its forthcoming fiery visit to Sagittarius. While the flashiness of the shower varies, it always adds a burst of brightness to the spirit while promoting authenticity, blunt honesty, and sociability. This month, be kind to your immune system by aligning with the rhythm of the season: be sure to stay warm, stay positive, get plenty of rest, and keep your environment ordered, attractive, and bright.

Tess Whitehurst

November 1

Wednesday

2nd ♓

☽ → ♈ 2:43 am

Color of the day: Topaz
Incense of the day: Marjoram

All Saints' Day

Dance in the Graveyard

Did you know that by the turn of the 1800s, cemeteries were no longer just places for the dead, but also community parks meant to be visited and walked in? They were even places to hold picnics and other gatherings.

On this day, remember with joy your loved ones who've passed on by visiting them in the graveyard. Tidy their gravesites if needed, smile, and remember their time on earth with you. Honor your ancestors. Sprinkle a mixture of red rose petals (love), yellow rose petals (I will never forget you), rosemary (remembrance), and ivy (friendship) on the gravesite before leaving. And yes, it's totally okay to talk to your loved one at their gravesite. If you don't have loved ones buried close by, why not adopt a neglected-looking burial site at the nearest cemetery?

Laurel Reufner

November 2

Thursday

2nd ♈

☽ v/c 11:03 pm

Color of the day: White
Incense of the day: Clove

Magic Media Diet

Every day we consume huge amounts of data: news, information, education, commercials, stories, and tons of both useful and useless stuff. It resonates within us, creating perceptions and reality. With the sun in Scorpio now, the sign known for the 1960s catchphrase "Turn on, tune in, drop out," it's a great time to go on a magical media diet.

For one day, turn off the TV, resist the radio, avoid newspapers and online news sites, and don't even read the blogs or Twitter feeds you follow. By dropping out of consuming outside media, you will turn on the inside imagination station and tune in to your own creative images. You never know what magic will bubble to the surface. Freed of outside images, our own images arise. We are inspired to create, express, and attune…to ourselves. If magic is "the power to transform energy at will," then this indeed is magic.

Dallas Jennifer Cobb

 November 3
Friday

2nd ♈
☽ → ♉ 5:46 am

Color of the day: Purple
Incense of the day: Rose

A Spell to Prepare Your home for Spirits

Today, Mercury is resting well in the sign of Scorpio, adding increased awareness of the spirit world and opening the lines of communication between our realm and those of our allies. With the sun also transiting Scorpio and the moon dancing momentarily in Taurus, the conditions are right for you to find spirits in your home, especially the beloved dead.

Prepare for them by cleaning your home like you do when company is coming. Set out a bowl of milk, a glass of wine or juice, a cup of coffee, and a few snacks. Light a white candle, and as you do so, set the space by saying:

From under and over, from within and without, from behind and before, I open the door. Spirits, join me, if you are of good will. I've set this space for you to fill!

Allow the candle to burn safely for several hours.

Devin hunter

November 4
Saturday

2nd ♉
Full Moon 1:23 am

Color of the day: Black
Incense of the day: Magnolia

The hand of Fate

Using a lump of blue clay, sculpt a hand, copying the shape, size, and identifying details of one of your own hands. Carefully include your palm lines, and incorporate any planetary or elemental symbols you'd like to use to enrich your spell. Place this on a base of sesame seeds. Finally, insert a birthday cake candle into each sculpted fingertip. As you light each candle, say the following incantation:

Fortuitous fate, intervene; ensure my adaptive reasoning.

Let all five candles burn down completely, then wrap this powerful spell in a black cloth and hide it in a secret location. Sprinkle the sesame seeds and any wax drippings at the doors and windows of your home to seal them with the fortification of the hand of fate. Keep it clandestine, keep it safe.

Estha McNevin

November 5
Sunday

3rd ♉

☽ v/c 4:29 am

☽ → ♊ 5:26 am

Color of the day: Yellow
Incense of the day: Almond

**Daylight Saving Time
ends at 2:00 a.m.**

You have a Special hour Today

Daylight saving time ended at
2:00 o'clock this morning by
giving us back the hour it stole from
us last spring. We can think of today
as a 25-hour day. What are you going
to do with that extra hour? You don't
need to wake up at 2:00 a.m. to celebrate. Instead, give yourself an hour
in which you don't have to meet anyone else's expectations. A tarot spread
can help you decide what to do.

Begin with card I, the Magician.
That's you today. What magic can
you do today? Lay card II, the High
Priestess, next to card I. She's a trust-
worthy advisor. Listen to her voice as
you shuffle the minor arcana cards.
Let her guide you as you lay out three
or four cards. What is she saying?
Finish your spread with card VII, the
Chariot. What is the path of your
tarot journey today?

Barbara Ardinger

November 6
Monday

3rd ♊

Color of the day: Silver
Incense of the day: Hyssop

Stop the Gossip Spell

If you can, perform this spell on a
windy night when heavy clouds
scud across the sky and the wind
rattles the shutters. You'll need an
old white T-shirt you've worn, a gray
candle, a sheet of paper, and a pen.
Light the candle and write the gossip
on the paper. Turn the T-shirt inside
out and lay it flat. Hold the paper over
the T-shirt and tear it into bits. Now
tie up all the corners of the T-shirt
into a bundle. Blow out the candle.
In secret, go to a secluded area. Here,
you'll bury the T-shirt and paper. As
you bury the bundle, say these words
with conviction:

Gossip, rumors, lies, and plot,

Lie in this earthly grave and rot!

Tell no one about this and the gossip
will soon stop.

James Kambos

November 7
Tuesday

3rd ♊

☽ v/c 5:40 am

☽ → ♋ 5:45 am

Color of the day: Scarlet
Incense of the day: Ylang-ylang

Election Day (general)

Banish Evil Politicians

It's Election Day! A waning moon helps banish the unwanted. This spell banishes evil or corrupt politicians/political behavior.

Choose a local election or an issue that concerns you.

Do this spell early in the day, when or before the polls first open.

Get a map that includes the area affected, whether a state, county, or school district, plus an orange marker (color of leadership) and a handful of whole barley.

Burn a purifying incense, such as sage or frankincense.

Point your wand or athame at each item you'll use, one at a time, saying:

I consecrate this (name of item) by the powers of the Gods, to work my will in banishing evil from (election/issue).

On the map, outline the area of concern in orange marker. As you do so, repeat:

Evil be gone, evil be gone.

Now place the barley over the orange outline, repeating the same phrase:

Evil be gone, evil be gone.

Then say:

So mote it be!

Leave the map on your altar until after election results are in.

Deborah Lipp

NOTES:

November 8
Wednesday

3rd ♋

Color of the day: Brown
Incense of the day: Lilac

Banish Negativity

As we move into the darker months, it is good to let go of whatever negativity we have been holding on to, so we don't drag it into the dark with us. This spell will help you do that.

In a dim, quiet room (or outside at night), light one black candle and one white candle. Meditate for a moment on what things in your life lift you up and which ones pull you down. Then concentrate on the black candle and say this spell:

Quietly and willingly

I let go

Of all those things that no longer work for my benefit

And let the light shine in,

Even during the darker months.

I let go of negativity.

I let it go

And welcome the positive instead.

Then blow out the black candle and spend a few minutes enjoying the glow of the white one.

Deborah Blake

November 9
Thursday

3rd ♋
☽ v/c 12:14 am
☽ → ♌ 7:29 am

Color of the day: Turquoise
Incense of the day: Carnation

Banish It!

It's banishing time. Now is the time to clear out, clean out, and let go of things that no longer serve you. Use this spell to clear away the clutter.

You will need a sheet of brown paper, some white thread, and a pen.

Center and ground yourself. Focus on that which you seek to banish. In the center of the brown paper, draw a large banishing pentagram. A banishing pentagram is a five-pointed star that starts in the bottom-left corner.

Draw a circle around your five-pointed star. Write your thoughts inside the pentacle. When finished, fold the paper away from you.

Tie nine knots in the white thread. Tie the paper with the white thread. To complete the spell, burn the packet in a fire-safe dish and discard the ashes in a trash receptacle away from your home.

Najah Lightfoot

November 10

Friday

3rd ♌

4th Quarter 3:36 pm

Color of the day: Rose

Incense of the day: Vanilla

Shelter from the Storm

Have you ever stood under an evergreen tree in a rainstorm? Thanks to the arrangement of boughs and needles, very little rain falls underneath the tree itself, leaving the ground below almost dry. Instead, the rain runs down the boughs and drips at the tree's root line, nourishing it while protecting the trunk from wet and rot.

Stop for a moment and consider those things in your life that both protect and nourish you. These might be as concrete as a roof overhead and a regular job or as esoteric as your family's love or the protection of a deity. Consider how each item provides shelter.

Make a list of those aspects of your daily existence that shelter you from life's storms and keep you safe and well. Tape the list to your bathroom mirror. Each morning, as you face the new day, read the list aloud and say:

I am grateful for shelter from life's storms.

Susan Pesznecker

November 11

Saturday

4th ♌

☽ v/c 3:55 am

☽ → ♍ 11:41 am

Color of the day: Gray

Incense of the day: Sandalwood

Veterans Day

A Remembrance

On this day, we honor all the warriors who have served our countries and kept us safe from harm.

We probably have family and/or friends who have served in the armed forces, and we should thank them for the work they have done on our behalf. Give them a hug, thank them for their service, and make it clear that you support their efforts and their service. Ask your gods to bless them for their service.

What makes our US veterans special is they choose to serve, so they should be supported in every way. Take some time today to write to your government representatives and tell them to be sure to keep veterans benefits from being cut. Tell them that veterans deserve even more. What price can you put on our safety and security? Veterans would have paid the ultimate price if needed. We should do the same for them.

Boudica

November 12

Sunday

4th ♏

Color of the day: Gold
Incense of the day: Eucalyptus

Send a Message to the Dead

Many Witches work intimately with the Beloved and Mighty Dead. Here is a spell that works with the wind to establish a connection with a particular person who has passed over.

Place a glass of fresh water and a white candle surrounded by a ring of angelica root in front of an image or a possession of this Beloved Dead. Ground and center and begin to enter trance in your way. Light the white candle and dedicate the water and the angelica root to the person. Listen and open with all your senses as you sincerely implore this spirit to contact you.

When you are ready, go to a window or door in the western part of your home, open it, and whistle through it into the air. Let the whistle channel the intention into the Otherworld and straight to the Beloved Dead. Repeat this over a series of nights.

Gede Parma

November 13

Monday

4th ♏

☽ v/c 10:45 am
☽ → ♎ 6:26 pm

Color of the day: White
Incense of the day: Clary sage

Banish Illness

To help yourself (or a loved one) recover or heal from illness or injury, use this spell—along with proper medical treatment, of course.

Anoint a large white candle with eucalyptus essential oil and light it. If you wish, you can also add a few drops of the oil to the pool of melted wax that forms around the wick. Visualize the illness in a specific place on or in the body. See it dissolving, fading. Imagine your will as a strong wind blowing away the illness like a fog. Chant:

Illness be gone, no more a threat.

Illness be gone, I will forget

That your presence here was ever allowed.

Illness be gone, dissolve like a cloud.

Repeat this process every day as desired by extinguishing and relighting the candle, or just let the candle burn out.

Ember Grant

November 14

Tuesday

4♏ ♎

Color of the day: Maroon
Incense of the day: Geranium

The Iron Maiden

Procure a large, used plastic kewpie doll's head and twenty-three rusty nails. Carefully poke each nail through the flesh of the doll's face, from the inside out. As you do so, incant the following and ask the doll's head to watch over and protect you from a specific enemy:

*Kewpie gri, watch over me, absorb
this hex of hate from (name of enemy).
Kewpie gri, da abbo bo mi.*

If you are able to, acquire a photo or write the name of the person you need protection from on a small piece of black paper and place it inside the head of the doll. Hang this in a hidden place on your property and keep its existence to yourself. Upon completion, give a thankful eulogy to your kewpie gri. Make a small coffin and bury this powerful spell deep in a marked and honored grave adorned with living flowers.

Estha McNevin

November 15

Wednesday

4♏ ♎

☽ v/c 7:50 pm

Color of the day: Yellow
Incense of the day: Bay laurel

Check Your Crown Spell

The energies swelling in the air today bring forth an awareness of your vital life force and sense of freedom. In my spiritual tradition, Sacred Fires, we use the symbol of the crown as a tool to represent both of these things as well as our own personal sovereignty in life. Today is the perfect day for you to check to see if you're still wearing your crown and to make any adjustments necessary to maintain its presence.

This morning or night when the clock strikes 11:11, take a few moments to align your energy with the universe and to draw down your sacred crown of power. Place your right hand over your heart and your left hand over your right pectoral muscles, then take three deep breaths and chant:

*Serpent rising, owl descend,
spider weaving with no end!*

Chant this until you feel all of your energy become centered on the now.

Devin Hunter

November 16

Thursday

4th ♎︎

☽ → ♏︎ 3:19 am

Color of the day: Green
Incense of the day: Balsam

Autumnal Airing

Perhaps there is no able-bodied person in your immediate household to do heavy lifting or climbing. Make the annual fall clean-up a family affair. When the younger relatives arrive, distribute the chores and tools. Many hands make light work. Clean the front yard, back yard, patio, and porch. Wash the windows, inside and out, and clear away any cobwebs in high and low corners. Dust the ceiling fans and chandeliers, and move the furniture for a thorough vacuuming. Wash all the linens, both table and bed. Run little-used bakeware, utensils, and glassware through the dishwasher.

In no time, your domicile will be sparkling. Have the elders prepare the meals, and gather everyone together to break bread. Serve a light meal at lunch to fortify everyone for the remainder of the day and a heartier repast when all is done. An alternative might be to accomplish all of the above for a member of your community who is in need of assistance.

Emyme

November 17

Friday

4th ♏︎

Color of the day: Purple
Incense of the day: Alder

Spirit Clearing Spell

The element of spirit concerns the mind and the soul. Spirit magic deals in the subtleties of life. It is common to pick up bits of negativity and other distractions during the day. Spirit magic can help to release those.

For this spell, you will need a black bowl and a white bowl, plus a handful of clear crystal beads. Start with your beads in the white bowl. Stir them with your hand and let your thoughts wander. When you come to a troublesome thought, pick up a bead. Acknowledge the thought, then let it go, dropping the bead in the black bowl. Black is the color of binding, so it works for holding things you wish to release. Continue the process until you run out of thoughts that bother you.

After you finish the spell, rinse the beads under running water. Then let them dry, ready to reuse another time.

Elizabeth Barrette

November 18

Saturday

4th ♏

☽ v/c 6:42 am

New Moon 6:42 am

☽ → ♐ 1:59 pm

Color of the day: Indigo

Incense of the day: Sage

Scorpio Self-Mastery

A new moon is a time of new beginnings and invites us to set intentions that will grow as the moon swells to full on December 3rd. Today's new moon is in the fixed water sign of Scorpio, the sign of bonding, control, and intensity. It is a powerful spiritual and sexual energy, transformative in nature. Scorpio is passionate, perceptive, and focused, so let's set an intention for self-mastery. Where are your passions, and which of them needs focus? Set an intention there, such as:

I love to write poetry and want to devote more time to it.

Make your intention SMART—specific, measurable, achievable, results-focused, and time-bound:

I will write poetry, longhand, after breakfast, one page a day, so that by the full moon I will have fifteen pages, or fifteen poems in total.

Now get to work and manifest what you have set out to create.

Dallas Jennifer Cobb

November 19

Sunday

1st ♐

Color of the day: Amber

Incense of the day: Hyacinth

Magickal Tablecloth

S elect or sew a light- or neutral-colored tablecloth that is made of cotton or a cotton blend, is not too bulky, and fits your favorite table. Use the tablecloth for meals, rituals, or other important gatherings. Afterward, give each guest or participant a permanent ink pen to write on the tablecloth, signing their name and adding a date and perhaps a comment, a sketch, a design, or whatever inspires them.

After they leave, trace over their work with a fine-point permanent marker, then embroider the tracings with brightly colored embroidery floss for permanence. The tablecloth will become a growing memento of important occasions as well as a gathering point for magick and memories.

To use your magickal table cover, lay the decorated cloth over the table with reverence and ceremony. Reflect on the energies within, saying:

All these people, all these times, all these intentions, be here with me now.

Susan Pesznecker

November 20

Monday

1st ♐

☽ v/c 7:26 pm

Color of the day: Ivory
Incense of the day: Lily

Good Sleep Spell

Many of us struggle to get a decent night's sleep. It can be hard to turn off our brain after a long and hectic day. It can sometimes help to tuck a lavender pillow under your pillow. You can write out this spell and put it inside one, or say it right before bed:

Gentle goddess of the night,

Who fades the day and dims the light,

Grant me safe and peaceful rest

That I might rise again refreshed

With naught but gentle peaceful dreams,

Cradled in your moon's soft beams.

Deborah Blake

November 21

Tuesday

1st ♐

☽ → ♑ 2:14 am

☉ → ♐ 10:05 pm

Color of the day: Red
Incense of the day: Cedar

Summon a Spirit Spell

This spell will help you communicate with the deceased. You should perform this ritual with respect. You'll need some white sage, a small bell, a magic mirror, and a white candle in a holder. Begin by casting a protective circle and burning the sage. On a table or altar, place the bell, mirror, and candle. Light the candle and gently ring the bell three times. Call the deceased by name, and ask if they'd contact you through the mirror. Say:

(Name of the deceased), if you can leave death's gentle embrace,

Please show me your face.

The mirror may mist over, then watch for the deceased's face to appear. They may look younger than you remember. Quietly ask any questions; their responses will be gestures. Then thank them and let them go. Ring the bell again, clear the circle, and snuff out the candle. If this didn't work, try again. Keep your sessions short.

James Kambos

November 22
Wednesday

1st ♑

Color of the day: White
Incense of the day: Lavender

A happy holidays Charm

The holiday season can be full of fun or turmoil, often both. We have many tasks to do, and most of us spend time with our families. It helps to get a handle on the hectic times with some common sense and a little magic. Here are some practical tips.

Plan your schedule in advance. Make your most important commitments first, then plan around them. Take breaks as needed. Do fun things with family. Remember, it's okay to say no.

For this spell, you will need a strand of thread and some mixed beads, with which you can make a bracelet or other charm. Choose a bead for each of your relatives. As you thread each bead onto the strand, picture a happy memory with that person and concentrate on making happiness the focus of your time together. When you finish stringing all the beads, knot the strand and keep it with you.

Elizabeth Barrette

November 23
Thursday

1st ♑

☽ v/c 5:33 am

☽ → ♒ 3:14 pm

Color of the day: Crimson
Incense of the day: Jasmine

Thanksgiving Day

Southern Welcome

The pineapple has long been a sign of hospitality and generosity in the Southern United States. Bring that symbolism, and its attendant energies, into your own home.

For this spell, you'll need an image of a pineapple (I found my pineapple mandala online) and your favorite coloring tools. You'll also need a frame. As you color your image, mentally see your home as more open and welcoming, a place where friends old and new enjoy hanging out. When finished, frame your picture and hang it near the door to your home. Anoint the edges of the frame monthly with a welcoming oil, such as lemon.

Laurel Reufner

November 24

Friday

1st ♒

Color of the day: Coral
Incense of the day: Thyme

Write a Letter to Santa

Today is traditionally the beginning of the holiday season. Santa Claus, with his Pagan origins, is the spirit of generosity. He lets us be in touch with our inner child, and ask for what we want from a place of innocence. On your altar, set up the following items:

- The Nine of Cups card (the "wish card") from a tarot deck

- A pen

- A sheet of paper

- A stamped envelope

- Symbols of the four elements (for example, a feather for air, a candle for fire, a cup of water for water, and a stone for earth)

- An image of Santa

Meditate on the Nine of Cups card, asking yourself what is it you truly want.

Touch the pen, paper, and envelope to each elemental symbol, saying:

By (air/fire/water/earth), may gifts come to me when they are asked for by my true self.

Begin your letter by writing "Dear Santa," and ask for sincerely desired gifts. Let go of any wishes that are momentary, faddish, or whimsical. Consider what you really want and need. Seal the letter in the envelope, saying:

So mote it be!

Mail the letter to Santa at the North Pole.

Deborah Lipp

Notes:

November 25
Saturday

1st ♒

☽ v/c 9:37 pm

Color of the day: Blue
Incense of the day: Rue

Savings Spell

Are you one of those people who has trouble saving things—money, for instance? Or maybe you find yourself wasting time and would like to manage it better. Maybe you can't seem to stop at just one brownie. If you need help making things last, here's a spell to help you conserve.

Find something to use as a symbol of what you wish to save. You could use a coin to represent money or a clock to symbolize time, or use a picture of the object. Designate a place where you will store the symbol—a special box, for example. Visualize managing this item, and see your desired outcome. Keep the box in a place where you can see it but not easily reach it, such as on a high shelf. Use these words to seal the spell:

Help me manage, help me save,

Conserve the item that I crave.

Keep this resource safe and sound,

So there's enough to go around.

Ember Grant

November 26
Sunday

1st ♒

☽ → ♓ 3:04 am

2nd Quarter 12:03 pm

Color of the day: Gold
Incense of the day: Frankincense

Sacred Sexuality

Times change and social standards change. What was risque twenty years ago is old hat today, as we as a society work to heal what patriarchy, misogyny, and Christianity did to sex.

Today, celebrate sex as sacred and make time to get in touch with your own sacred sexuality. Spend time alone caring for your body—moisturizing, shaving, massaging, and pampering. As you do so, let yourself come alive in your own sexuality, fantasizing and dreaming about sacred sex—not the type of sex that you have been told is correct by society and not what you see on TV or in magazines, but your own deep desires: sensual and sexual.

Put on soft clothing and dance alone in front of a mirror while invoking the goddesses of sacred sexuality: Aphrodite, Inanna, Magdalene, and Lilith. Know how lovely you are.

Dallas Jennifer Cobb

November 27

Monday

2nd ♓

Color of the day: Lavender
Incense of the day: Neroli

Cleanse and Protect Your Vehicle

Everyone loves a new car. But before you get your new wheels on the road, have you thought about cleansing and protecting your new ride? We know energy attaches itself to things. Even if you are the first owner of your car, others still drove your car around the factory and to the dealership. And if you bought your car used, there's no telling how many others drove your vehicle before you became its owner.

To cleanse your car, fill a spray bottle with three pinches of salt and two cups of water. Spray the inside and outside of your car. Next, light a sage bundle and smudge your entire car, inside and out, while saying a prayer for protection and safe travel. Snuff out the sage bundle when you have finished blessing your car. Now you can travel with confidence.

Najah Lightfoot

November 28

Tuesday

2nd ♓

☽ v/c 7:09 am
☽ → ♈ 11:30 am

Color of the day: Gray
Incense of the day: Bayberry

Rune of the Sun Spell of Success

The Nordic rune of the sun is sometimes known as Sowilo and looks like a lightning strike (⚡). It represents triumph, success, and the sun itself. I like to make the sound sss and trace or draw this rune when working for success.

Perform this spell either at dawn while the sun is rising in the east or in the middle of the day with the sun strong overheard. Carve the Sowilo rune into a gold candle seven times. Light the candle, then begin to rock back and forth and start to make the sound sss. Let the sound overwhelm your consciousness as you feel yourself coated in golden sunlight and opening every cell to its power. When you feel the peak of that solar force within you, release the charge into the candle and pinch out the flame. Light the candle when you need to work for victory.

Gede Parma

November 29
Wednesday

2nd ♈

Color of the day: Brown
Incense of the day: Lilac

The Single Traveler

I observe a tradition of travel in the autumn, some quiet time alone for reflection. A set of actions makes the hotel room my own. Feel free to incorporate these into your own travels.

Open or close the drapes, whichever is appropriate. No matter how short a time you plan to be there, unpack and air out your clothing. Fill the ice bucket, and place perishables in the mini-fridge. Place any books and personal items on the extra bed or a desk. Set all toiletries on the bathroom vanity. Do all of this in a careful, mindful way—not haphazard, but with the intention of clearing out the energy of previous inhabitants. When checking out, be sure to leave a gratuity for the housekeeping staff. This builds goodwill and good luck for future travels.

Travels take me far and wide,

Hearth and house are left aside.

A few days of a simpler life,

Less clutter, less noise, less strife,

In this temporary home for me.

As I write, so mote it be.

Emyme

November 30
Thursday

2nd ♈

☽ v/c 1:37 pm
☽ → ♉ 3:38 pm

Color of the day: Turquoise
Incense of the day: Mulberry

A Winter Nap

We're in the deepest, darkest days of winter now, and across most of the land our furry, feathery, finny, and leafy cousins are asleep and building up the energy they'll need when they awaken in the spring. A long winter nap is good for us, too. See if you can fit a nap into your schedule today.

Visualize yourself in a cozy place underground, a barrow or a cave. Look around. Who is sharing the space with you? Greet the hibernating animals and wish them well, and do the same with any roots you see hanging down. Now watch as gnomes and dwarves and others who specialize in things northerly and wintery enter the space. Their leader is Sylvanus, elder god of forests and plains. Greet these ancient guardians of the land and ask what you can do to help them tend the land. Vow to work with them all through the year.

Barbara Ardinger

December

December, in the minds of many, is both the quintessential winter month and one of the busiest months of the year. It is a month full of joyous celebrations from many traditions. Advent, Bodhi Day, Saturnalia, Kwanzaa, Pancha Ganapati, Christmas, Hanukkah, and Yule are just a small selection of festivals that have their calendrical home in the month of December.

The themes of light (literal, energetic, and metaphorical), wisdom, and goodwill are a common thread among many of the celebrations. This is a good time of year to remember that despite our differences, we have much in common with one other. In a modern culture where many of us practice religious and spiritual pluralism to some degree, December presents more than one holy festival for each of us to nurture our spirit.

In the Northern Hemisphere, the winter solstice marks the official start of winter—a season of introspection. Though the land appears outwardly to be in a quiet slumber, we know that beneath the soil, down in the roots and in the dens of animals, there is a process of incubative growth occurring. Once again, the seasons of our soul align in harmony with the seasons of nature.

Blake Octavian Blair

December 1
Friday

2nd ♉

☽ v/c 8:53 pm

Color of the day: Pink
Incense of the day: Orchid

The happy hearth

At the center of every home is a hearth: a fireplace, a wood-burning stove, a central furnace, or perhaps a kitchen range. Each represents the traditionally protective, nourishing fire at every home's center.

Treat your hearth to a winter cleansing. Clean your fireplace or oven or replace a used furnace filter. Clear away dust and grit, and polish with nontoxic cleanser and a clean rag.

Magickally cleanse your hearth using the elements. Use saltwater (earth + water) to trace a plus sign or the Algiz rune (ᛉ) on the hearth for protection and opportunity. Smudge or use incense (air + fire) of cedar, sage, or juniper for purification.

Light a fire in the hearth or turn on the oven or furnace. Meditate on the light and warmth, saying:

I am grateful for the gifts this hearth provides. May I always find peace and safety here.

Enjoy your fire—or bake cookies in your freshened oven!

Susan Pesznecker

December 2
Saturday

2nd ♉

☽ → ♊ 4:21 pm

Color of the day: Blue
Incense of the day: Ivy

Saturn's Blessings

Saturday is ruled by Saturn, whom astrologers call the taskmaster of life, the teacher of the hard lessons in our lives. Saturnus is one of the oldest Roman gods, originally a ruler of fertility (in both fields and households), wealth, and periodic renewal. Although his lessons can seem challenging, there's no need to be afraid of this god. Keep the idea of renewal in mind.

If you are facing a hard lesson or have recently learned a hard lesson, invoke Saturn for help:

Mighty Saturn, Lord of Karma, I thank you for lessons that have taught me to be a better person. [Name at least one of these lessons.] As a strict but fair teacher, please guide me along the path through the next lesson I know is coming to me. [Name the possible future lesson.] I give thanks for your blessings that sometimes come in disguise.

Barbara Ardinger

December 3

Sunday

2nd ♊

☽ Full Moon 10:47 am

Color of the day: Amber
Incense of the day: Marigold

help with Change

It's that time of year when we begin to slow down. The year is almost at an end and the weather gets colder. In some areas, most of the leaves are off the trees and the landscape is looking bare.

This moon we are reminded that another change is coming. This coming cycle is part of the circle of life, death, and rebirth. As with all cycles, we should be prepared to deal with changes. We ask our chosen deities to help us to adjust to change. Some of us love the coming season, but for others it may be a season of trials. Holidays are hard for some, while others revel in the planning and preparation. This season can be a joyful memory in the making or it can be a painful memory.

Whatever your ability is to deal with change, we can all use some help. We are reminded this moon that it is okay to ask for help when we need it. Whether it's from our gods, those we love, or professionals, we should never be afraid to ask for help when dealing with change.

Boudica

December 4

Monday

3rd ♊

☽ v/c 2:13 pm

☽ → ♋ 3:37 pm

Color of the day: Silver
Incense of the day: Narcissus

Grains of Saint Barbara

Some folks start wheat seeds growing on this day, in celebration of Saint Barbara. If the grain is growing well by Christmas, then the coming year's crop will be a good one.

Try your own take on this custom by starting some heathy greens for your Yule table today. Broccoli, radishes, and beets are all good options for growing microgreens indoors. Or, if you have the equipment, try sprouting some slow-starting seeds instead. Whatever you decide to grow, ask it to bring you luck and prosperity in the coming year—your "good harvest." Serve the microgreens or sprouts as part of your holiday meal.

Laurel Reufner

December 5

Tuesday

3rd ♋

Color of the day: Maroon
Incense of the day: Ginger

Shh!

Use this spell to stop gossip. Get two squares of cork no smaller than two inches square. Its soundproofing qualities will silence rumors. You will also need a pen, a yellow sheet of paper, and some string or tape.

At your altar, burn cloves in a censer, or burn a stick of clove incense. Pass each ingredient (cork, paper, pen, string) through the smoke, saying each time:

No unkind words may be spoken about me.

No untrue words may be spoken about me.

No rumor shall spread.

So mote it be!

On the yellow paper, write rumors you've heard about yourself. If you aren't sure, use phrases like "Have you heard about (your name)?" Fill one side of the page.

Fold each side of the paper into the center, then fold it over again. As you fold, concentrate on sealing away these words so they cannot be spoken.

Place the paper between the pieces of cork, then tie the bundle with string or seal it with tape.

Say:

Silence blesses me! So mote it be!

Hide this spell in a dark corner of a closet. You can leave it there indefinitely.

Deborah Lipp

Notes:

December 6

Wednesday

3rd ♋

☽ v/c 12:56 pm

☽ → ♌ 3:37 pm

Color of the day: White
Incense of the day: Lavender

Teachers

As the year comes to a close, take a moment to reflect upon those who have been your teachers. A teacher does not always take the form of a human being. Teachers can be animals, plants, things, or spirits.

Teachers teach by example. They can teach us how to move forward successfully, or, by their negative examples, they can help us choose a better path. Either way, we learn something.

Non-humans are teachers too. We learn patience through working with plants in our garden. We learn how to trust in the cycle of death and rebirth through the change of seasons. We can learn the value of a simple oil change if we fail to care for our vehicle.

Take a moment to reflect on who and what have been your teachers this year. Bless the good ones with love and thank the ones who taught you through adversity.

Najah Lightfoot

 December 7

Thursday

3rd ♌

Color of the day: Green
Incense of the day: Clove

A holiday Peace Spell

As you socialize and entertain this holiday season, some of the friends and family you'll mingle with won't share your spiritual beliefs. Many Pagans face this situation every December. Before you entertain, fill your home with positive vibrations by using this spell.

Dress a lavender-scented candle with olive oil. Light it and carry it throughout your home as you say:

Peace and tolerance dwell here.

All are welcome here.

I welcome every guest.

All will be treated with respect.

Hang mistletoe wherever you can. It's not only seasonal, but also a great purifying herb. If you have a fireplace, burn some mistletoe with the wood to banish all negativity. To keep things calm, try to avoid using red candles, and instead go with green and gold. Those colors keep things grounded. If someone is irritating, think of this spell. Who knows, you may even be polite to your nosy Aunt Edith!

James Kambos

December 8
Friday

3rd ♌

☽ v/c 5:40 pm

☽ → ♍ 6:09 pm

Color of the day: Rose
Incense of the day: Mint

Elemental Protection

The darker, colder months can leave us feeling more vulnerable. This is a simple protection spell that calls on the elements for help. It can be used all year round whenever you feel like you need it.

Light a black or white candle and visualize a strong wall being formed around you from each element in turn.

Power of air, protect me with the force of the winter gale and the summer breeze.

Power of water, protect me with the might of ocean waves and rushing waterfall.

Power of fire, protect me with the glory of the roaring bonfire.

Power of earth, protect me with the steady strength of the ground below my feet.

I am protected. I am safe. I thank you.

Deborah Blake

 # December 9
Saturday

3rd ♍

Color of the day: Black
Incense of the day: Pine

Altar Cleansing

Sometimes as a result of our busy lives, our altars become neglected and covered with dust or clutter. Take some time to remove all the items and clean them as well as the altar itself. Clean physically and magically. Remove dust and dirt first, and clean all your objects and tools. Then perform a cleansing ritual.

Create a cleansing "potion" by adding a few drops of lemon juice to a cup of warm water. Put the lemon water in a spray bottle and add a clear quartz crystal. Also add a grain of salt, if desired (saltwater can damage some surfaces).

Spray this mixture lightly on everything, then dry with a soft cloth. Visualize the space and objects being refreshed and renewed for their purposes. Chant as you clean:

This space is clean, the objects too,

With the water, all renew.

Unwanted energy dispel,

With these words, all be well.

Ember Grant

December 10

Sunday

3rd ♍

4th Quarter 2:51 am

☽ v/c 10:02 pm

Color of the day: Orange
Incense of the day: Juniper

Independence Spell

With the moon currently in Virgo, the sun in Sagittarius, and winter settling in, you are likely to be a bit more aware today of your personal relationships and the impact they have on you. Perhaps what is most important today is that you see yourself as an independent person, and that you consider the aspects of your relationships that either support or hinder your independence.

Take a piece of black construction paper and draw a pentacle on it in white chalk. On the inside of the star, write your complete name, and then at each point, write one word that you feel describes an aspect of independence you wish to see enter your life. Take a few deep breaths, and with your pointer finger, trace the pentacle. As you pass through each point, say aloud the word that you wrote there. Do this nine times, increasing in speed and volume each time. When complete, place the paper in your Book of Shadows until you have obtained each aspect you summoned.

Devin Hunter

NOTES:

December 11

Monday

4th ♏

☽ → ♎ 12:01 am

Color of the day: Gray
Incense of the day: Rosemary

Bathtub Exorcism

For this spell, you will need:

- Bon Ami powder cleanser (or Bar Keepers Friend)
- 3 tablespoons asafoetida
- 13 drops pure essential frankincense oil
- ½ gallon distilled white vinegar
- Frankincense and myrrh incense
- A small white candle

Begin by thoroughly scrubbing your bathtub with Bon Ami. Combine the asafoetida, frankincense oil, and distilled white vinegar and shake this banishing mixture very well. Asperge the tub and any nearby tiles with the mixture as you demand the following:

Be gone, dark shadow; I command you, wonder not beyond your rent veil. Stay bound within your own dimension, for you are expelled from mine. Get out, uninvited host. Neither thief nor demonic foe will steal entry here. By my driven will, I banish thee with this

etheric alchemy. I fortify this space with light. With my right hand, I cast and seal a fiery pentacle. This consecration is complete. So mote it be.

Light the candle and incense inside the tub and leave the room to rest for twenty-four hours. Make sure the candle is in a safe, clean area, free of any overhanging flammable material.

Estha McNevin

NOTES:

December 12
Tuesday

4th ♎

Color of the day: Scarlet
Incense of the day: Ylang-ylang

Get Ready

With the moon in Libra today, it is a great time to focus on balance. Autumn has zoomed by, and we quickly approach the holiday season: Yule, Christmas, the New Year. It's time to attend to the details of our inner and outer lives, readying ourselves before we plunge into the weeks of merrymaking.

Today, tune in to the Libran energy of restoring balance. Take time to put your home in order. Sweep and mop. Throw in a load of laundry. Decorate your home for the festive season. Rearrange furniture and declutter. Attend to your altar, cleaning, clearing, and preparing it for Yule. Sweep the altar with a small bough of evergreen, cleansing and purifying. Light a candle and say:

I'm ready, my home's ready, my altar's ready, my heart's ready. I'm balanced and ready for the holidays. Time now to indulge in luxury.

Dallas Jennifer Cobb

December 13
Wednesday

4th ♎

☽ v/c 7:27 am
☽ → ♏ 8:59 am

Color of the day: Brown
Incense of the day: Marjoram

hanukkah begins

Call the Light Candle Spell

This spell will empower spells already cast and in process. It can also be used to shed light on a confusing situation.

Anoint a white candle with rosemary, myrrh, and rose oils. Anoint from the center of the candle to the top and then from the center to the base. Repeat this seven times. As you anoint the candle, become a channel of cosmic and limitless light as it flows through you and charges the candle. When you are ready, light the candle and briefly hold your hands above the flame and then bring them in a wave motion over your head, into your heart, and into your whole self to bring the magic. Let the candle burn down completely.

Gede Parma

December 14

Thursday

4th ♏

☽ v/c 8:42 pm

Color of the day: Turquoise
Incense of the day: Balsam

The Gift of Giving

Every year a few weeks before Christmas, it was tradition for my grandmother to create magick. She would set up a folding table in the spare room and wrap gifts. How special to watch as the tower of gifts grew! Much love and affection went into the decorative and clever wrapping she fashioned.

Should you wish to start such a tradition, or if this is currently a part of your holiday preparations, be sure to cleanse your workspace properly before you begin. Wash or wipe down the table or counter with a saltwater mixture. Smudge the room, the gifts, and the wrappings with sage. Play holiday music and perhaps allow yourself a glass of your favorite winter libation.

Although this may not seem like a traditional spell, when you are done, relax and close with cakes and ale.

Emyme

December 15

Friday

4th ♏

☽ → ♐ 8:07 pm

Color of the day: Coral
Incense of the day: Violet

Lemon Cupcake Day

Today is Lemon Cupcake Day. What's so special about lemon cupcakes?

As an herb, lemon has many uses. It is antibacterial and antifungal. It contains a lot of vitamin C, which explains its use in cold remedies. It also soothes throat irritation and supports the voice. In aromatherapy, lemon is cleansing and uplifting. It helps you wake up in the morning or cheer up if you feel down.

Cupcakes are lovely little treats. They're miniature cakes. You can indulge in a bit of sweetness without going overboard. They're cheap to buy and easy to find. If you bake your own, you can have a healthy dessert as well as a scrumptious one. Choose just the lemon cake for a mild effect. If you really want an herbal kick, fill the cake with lemon curd or soak it in lemon syrup or rosewater lemonade. Try your hand at kitchen witchery!

Elizabeth Barrette

December 16

Saturday

4♏ ↗

Color of the day: Gray
Incense of the day: Patchouli

Block-Removal Threshold Wash

Today, the moon, which has almost completed its cycle, resides in Sagittarius along with the sun, making it an excellent day for all forms of block removal. Harness the potency of the energy today by preparing ritual oils, incense, ointments, and herb blends for later use, and set time aside for meditation specific to this work.

In a saucepan, combine two cups water, the fresh peel of one lemon and one orange, and a handful of clove. Bring to a slight boil, then reduce the heat and simmer for nine minutes. As the mixture simmers, hold your hands over the pot and chant:

Ain't nothing gonna stand in my way,

Ain't nothing gonna keep me down!

Ain't no worries gonna steal my light,

Ain't no sorrow gonna make me cry!

When finished, let the mixture cool to room temperature. Strain the mixture and use the brew to wash the threshold of your front door.

Devin Hunter

December 17

Sunday

4th ♐

Color of the day: Yellow
Incense of the day: Heliotrope

Chakra Stone

Create a chakra stone by painting a column of color on your stone from root to crown (bottom to top). You will need a set of paints and brushes.

Go for a walk and find a stone that feels good when held in your hands.

With your paints set up and your stone before you, ground and center. When you feel calm, visualize your root, say *I have*, and paint a red dot near the bottom of your stone.

Visualize your groin, say *I feel*, and paint an orange dot above the red one.

Visualize your solar plexus, say *I will*, and paint a yellow dot above the other two, forming a vertical column of dots.

Visualize your heart, say *I love*, and paint a green dot.

Visualize your throat, say *I speak*, and paint a blue dot.

Visualize your third eye, say *I see*, and paint an indigo dot.

Visualize your crown, say *I know*, and paint a violet dot.

Breathe calm, balanced energy into the stone.

Hold the stone whenever you need help balancing or when you feel disconnected.

Deborah Lipp

NOTES:

☽ December 18
Monday

4th ♐

New Moon 1:30 am

☽ v/c 8:10 am

☽ → ♑ 8:33 am

Color of the day: White

Incense of the day: Clary sage

Note to Self Spell

The new moon is traditionally a time of contemplation and reflection. It's also a time for renewal. For this new moon, focus on either a project you'd like to begin or some aspect of your personal life that needs attention. Make a vow tonight to take the first steps to start that project or begin whatever you've been putting off—an exercise routine, for example, or opening a savings account. Write it down, and display the words in a place where you can see them every day. Decorate the space around your message—make this sacred space (you can even use your altar). To seal the spell, announce your plans aloud and finish with this chant:

Let these words reveal

My intention to begin.

Let me be inspired

Over and over again.

I will stay on track,

I will not look back.

Ember Grant

♥ December 19
Tuesday

1st ♑

Color of the day: Red

Incense of the day: Cinnamon

Honoring the Heart Protector

A new year is almost here. A dear friend of mine, Ravyn Stanfield, a sister Witch and a talented acupuncturist, taught me about the heart protector (aka the *pericardium*, the physical organ that surrounds the heart). In Traditional Chinese Medicine, the state of the heart protector is considered integral to overall wellness. To have no boundary around your heart is considered ill-advised; to have a closed heart is just as bad. Sometimes as a cycle comes to an end, we need to check in with our heart. Here is a simple spell to do that.

Ground and center and go for a walk in a place of natural beauty. If people move past you, notice them, make eye contact, and notice your heart. Notice the heart protector and feed it honey-like golden light. Open yourself to plants, trees, animals, birds, insects, fungi, stones, rivers, wind, light, etc. Each time you do this, notice your heart and its protector as well. Feel your grounding cord strongly rooted and firm, and breathe within the web of relationships.

Gede Parma

December 20

Wednesday

1st ⅛

☽ v/c 10:37 am

☽ → ≈ 9:29 pm

Color of the day: Topaz
Incense of the day: Bay laurel

hanukkah ends

Candle Care

Today is the last day of Hanukkah. Yule is upon us, and Christmas is just days away. Holiday celebrations for these and all religions and belief systems have one thing in common: the lighting of candles.

Candle magic is very dear to me. Practiced by the novice as well as the expert, it is part of every complicated ritual, yet it is as easy as lighting a candle and saying a blessing. Every candle lit by everyone the world over is a bit of magic, even if all it does is bring light. After all, what is more wonderful than bringing light to the dark?

Take some time to care for your candle collection. Trim wicks, clean out votive cups and candleholders, and replenish your stock. While doing so, remember to light a candle to bless your efforts:

*Candles, ancient and revered light
of the world,*

In all forms and colors,

For every season and reason,

Bring blessings upon me and my home.

Emyme

NOTES:

December 21

Thursday

1st ♒

☉ → ♑ 11:28 am

Color of the day: Crimson
Incense of the day: Myrrh

Yule – Winter Solstice

Give a Gift

Yule—the winter solstice—is an inspired time of year for many. Celebrate with gift giving, a powerful form of intentional magick. In giving a gift, we create intention, bring it to life by creating the gift, and pass this on to a loved one. The act of giving transmits magickal energy from one person to another, and the energy is magnified by the exchange.

The most powerful gifts are those we create with our own hands or spirit. Create a gift this season for a favorite friend or offer a gift of time, such as a lunch together, a promise of babysitting, or help with yard chores. As you package the gift, tie a green ribbon around it (for prosperity), saying:

Hey the gift, ho the gift, here the gift, there the gift. Now the time comes the gift, cheers may it bring!

Deliver the gift. As the ribbon is untied, the energy will release. Blessed be!

Susan Pesznecker

December 22

Friday

1st ♒

Color of the day: Pink
Incense of the day: Rose

Living Well Is the Best Revenge

We all have revenge fantasies, but it's true that living well is the best revenge. Today, shine forgiveness and compassion on an enemy, or someone you hold a grudge against, by letting your inner light shine. After last night, the longest night of the year, be in touch with your inner darkness. Know your shadow. Today, transform that darkness, lighting a light inside. Ask yourself:

How can I be happier, safer, healthier, and more peaceful?

Make a list. Change your mindset. Affirm:

I am blessed.

Take a small thing from your list and do it. Feel your internal energy shift, magically, with each small step taken toward self-mastery and self-care. Feel your inner light radiating. Shift your attention to someone outside of you, and let your light radiate out to them—lover, family, friend, or even enemy. Say:

He/She is happy, safe, healthy, and peaceful. All is well in _____'s world.

Dallas Jennifer Cobb

December 23

Saturday

1st ♒

☽ v/c 5:13 am

☽ → ♓ 9:42 am

Color of the day: Blue
Incense of the day: Sage

Wish Upon a Star

Print an image of your favorite version of trump XVII in the tarot, the Star. Hang this in the window of your bedroom before you turn in for the night. As you drift off to sleep, envision the star of Venus as a beautiful fairy queen. See her in your mind's eye drifting down from her celestial kingdom to hear your wish.

In a moment of composure, think about your heart's greatest desire and allow your spirit body to glow with the awareness of your purpose here on earth. Let the wand of Venus bless your nighttime journey as you contemplate the subconscious power of wishful thinking.

Use this exercise to learn how to believe in your own ability to achieve your goals, as you work to conjure them in accordance with your will.

Estha McNevin

December 24

Sunday

1st ♓

☽ v/c 9:48 pm

Color of the day: Gold
Incense of the day: Almond

Christmas Eve

Wish Upon a Star

Whether or not you celebrate Christmas, there is a certain magic in the air on Christmas Eve. Perhaps it is the potential for all those wishes being granted in the morning by a man who resembles the Holly King. Tap into that energy to make some wishes of your own, making sure to open yourself to whatever gifts the universe sends you.

For this spell, you can go outside and wish upon a star, use the star on the top of your tree, or simply draw a star on a piece of paper and then tuck it under your pillow. Light a white candle, if you like, and say:

> Tonight, on this magical mystical night,
>
> I wish for gifts, all shiny and bright,
>
> Gifts for the heart and gifts for the spirit,
>
> I send to the stars in the hope that they hear it.

Then say or think of your wishes.

Deborah Blake

December 25

Monday

1st ♓

☽ → ♈ 7:27 **pm**

Color of the day: Ivory
Incense of the day: Hyssop

Christmas Day

Candle Peace

We're now in the season of peace. Why not invite it to linger around your home into the coming new year with a decorative display for your space?

You'll need:

- A pretty glass dish (to contain all the ingredients)
- Lavender flowers or sprigs (peace)
- Birch bark pieces (blessings)
- Rose petals (calming)
- Lemon verbena (love)
- Cinnamon sticks (prosperity)
- 7–9 drops myrrh or frankincense essential or fragrance oil
- A white candle, such as a seven-day candle in a glass jar

In the glass bowl, mix your herbal elements together until you're happy with the proportions. I've deliberately left them out of these instructions since some of them depend on the size of the bits and pieces you choose to use. Add in the drops of oil. Place the candle in the middle of the pretty bowl and arrange the herbal mixture around it. Burn the candle once a day for seven days and thereafter as needed.

Laurel Reufner

NOTES:

December 26

Tuesday

1st ♈

2nd Quarter 4:20 am

Color of the day: White
Incense of the day: Cedar

Kwanzaa begins

Kwanzaa Broom Blessing

This is the beginning of Kwanzaa, a celebration of African and diaspora culture. Some of its roots come from harvest festivals. Part of that process involves not just picking the ripe crops but also clearing away the remains to let the fields rest before the new planting. That ties into the practice of vigorous housecleaning prior to the arrival of guests for the holidays. In this we see the principle of *Ujima*, collective work and responsibility.

Now is a good time for a broom blessing. Traditionally a broom is made from broomcorn, although it may also be made from twigs. A broom cleans both physically and metaphysically. Lay your new broom on your altar and say:

In the season of harvest,

We take up what is ripe

And we sweep away the chaff.

May this broom be consecrated

To clean and bless all that it touches.

Elizabeth Barrette

December 27

Wednesday

2nd ♈

☽ v/c 3:57 pm

Color of the day: Yellow
Incense of the day: Lilac

Give Me Strength!

Since you are smack in the middle of a potentially exhausting holiday season, now is a time for an energy spell.

Get a small red cloth about two inches square and a bright yellow ribbon. You're going to tie ten knots into the ribbon (ten is a number of energy), so make sure it's long enough. Place a red carnation on your altar.

Put a pinch of black tea and a shiny copper penny on the center of the cloth square.

Point your athame or wand at the ingredients, saying:

I am strong, I am full of energy,
I feel good.

(Improvise the words to match your particular needs this season.)

Use the ribbon to tie the cloth closed. As you tie each of the ten knots, say:

Strength and energy, so mote it be!

Carry your energy totem with you as you go about your busy day.

Deborah Lipp

December 28
Thursday

2nd ♈

☽ → ♉ 1:23 am

Color of the day: Green
Incense of the day: Nutmeg

When It's Time to Let Go

Every Pagan knows that the only constant on the planet is change. Everything evolves and revolves, but sometimes we don't want to ride along. That's when it's time to say, "I'm done." We do not, however, need to turn this affirmation into a Greek tragedy or a grand opera. Just make a simple statement:

I'm done.

Say it out loud. Say what you're done with. If a relationship or friendship has turned sour, say:

I'm done with (name of person).

If a project doesn't work anymore, say:

I'm done with this work.

Say it as a simple declarative sentence. When what you're done with pops back into your mind, say the statement again. Say it as often as necessary until the words seep into your mind and heart.

I'm done with this.

So mote it be.

Barbara Ardinger

December 29
Friday

2nd ♉

☽ v/c 9:01 am

Color of the day: Purple
Incense of the day: Yarrow

Enhancing Love

How can we make the love we share with others better? Love of family, love of friends, love of spouse—sometimes we take them for granted.

On your altar, place a pink or rose candle and pictures of your loved ones. Use rose oil (unless you are allergic) or a fragrance that brings to mind your loved ones. Remember the good times you've have and the trials that brought you closer.

Remembering what you have gone through in life with those you love is a great way to bring yourself closer to them. Tell them you love them and appreciate them. Give them your thanks for being there, and hold them close to you. These are the people who make your life meaningful. Tell them how much you appreciate them.

Boudica

December 30

Saturday

2nd ♉

☽ → ♊ 3:31 am

Color of the day: Indigo
Incense of the day: Rue

Wish Upon a Star

The old year thins away and once again we find ourselves looking at the past while being hopeful about the future. At this time of year, we have hopes and dreams of what we wish to accomplish in the future. This spell will help with that.

Perform this ritual in the evening. You'll need the Star card from the tarot and a bayberry-scented candle. Light the candle and lay the Star card before it. Look at the card; it's a symbol of hope and wishes. Now close your eyes and think of your wish. Place your hand on the card and draw it toward you. Visualize your wish coming true. Snuff out the candle and leave the card on your altar for a few days. Tonight, take a walk and think of your wish as you gaze at the stars.

James Kambos

December 31

Sunday

2nd ♊

☽ v/c 6:38 pm

Color of the day: Orange
Incense of the day: Eucalyptus

New Year's Eve

A Fresh New You

The year is almost over and congratulations are due. You've made it another 365 days as a human being on planet Earth. Considering all that life brings us, this is no small feat and deserves to be celebrated!

We each have our own way of celebrating New Year's Eve. Some gather with friends and large crowds of people, while others prefer a quiet evening at home. Before heading out or going to bed, take a cleansing bath. Add ¼ teaspoon eucalyptus essential oil to a half cup of sea salt. Add this mixture to two cups of water. Use the mixture in your bath or shower. Invoke a new beginning as you bathe:

Mysteries of old,

Mysteries of new,

I am cleansed and ready for you.

Blessed is the night,

Blessed is the dawn,

Blessed are we all year long!

Najah Lightfoot

Daily Magical Influences

Each day is ruled by a planet that possesses specific magical influences:

Monday (Moon): peace, healing, caring, psychic awareness, purification.

Tuesday (Mars): passion, sex, courage, aggression, protection.

Wednesday (Mercury): conscious mind, study, travel, divination, wisdom.

Thursday (Jupiter): expansion, money, prosperity, generosity.

Friday (Venus): love, friendship, reconciliation, beauty.

Saturday (Saturn): longevity, exorcism, endings, homes, houses.

Sunday (Sun): healing, spirituality, success, strength, protection.

Lunar Phases

The lunar phase is important in determining best times for magic.

The waxing moon (from the new moon to the full moon) is the ideal time for magic to draw things toward you.

The full moon is the time of greatest power.

The waning moon (from the full moon to the new moon) is a time for study, meditation, and little magical work (except magic designed to banish harmful energies).

Astrological Symbols

The Sun	☉	Aries	♈
The Moon	☽	Taurus	♉
Mercury	☿	Gemini	♊
Venus	♀	Cancer	♋
Mars	♂	Leo	♌
Jupiter	♃	Virgo	♍
Saturn	♄	Libra	♎
Uranus	♅	Scorpio	♏
Neptune	♆	Sagittarius	♐
Pluto	♇	Capricorn	♑
		Aquarius	♒
		Pisces	♓

The Moon's Sign

The moon's sign is a traditional consideration for astrologers. The moon continuously moves through each sign in the zodiac, from Aries to Pisces. The moon influences the sign it inhabits, creating different energies that affect our daily lives.

Aries: Good for starting things but lacks staying power. Things occur rapidly but quickly pass. People tend to be argumentative and assertive.

Taurus: Things begun now do last, tend to increase in value, and become hard to alter. Brings out an appreciation for beauty and sensory experience.

Gemini: Things begun now are easily changed by outside influence. Time for shortcuts, communications, games, and fun.

Cancer: Stimulates emotional rapport between people. Pinpoints need, supports growth and nurturance. Tend to domestic concerns.

Leo: Draws emphasis to the self, to central ideas or institutions, away from connections with others and emotional needs. People tend to be melodramatic.

Virgo: Favors accomplishment of details and commands from higher up. Focus on health, hygiene, and daily schedules.

Libra: Favors cooperation, compromise, social activities, beautification of surroundings, balance, and partnership.

Scorpio: Increases awareness of psychic power. Favors activities requiring intensity and focus. People tend to brood and become secretive under this moon sign.

Sagittarius: Encourages flights of imagination and confidence. This moon sign is adventurous, philosophical, and athletic. Favors expansion and growth.

Capricorn: Develops strong structure. Focus on traditions, responsibilities, and obligations. A good time to set boundaries and rules.

Aquarius: Rebellious energy. Time to break habits and make abrupt change. Personal freedom and individuality are the focus.

Pisces: The focus is on dreaming, nostalgia, intuition, and psychic impressions. A good time for spiritual or philanthropic activities.

Glossary of Magical Terms

Altar: A table that holds magical tools as a focus for spell workings.

Athame: A ritual knife used to direct personal power during workings or to symbolically draw diagrams in a spell. It is rarely, if ever, used for actual physical cutting.

Aura: An invisible energy field surrounding a person. The aura can change color depending on the state of the individual.

Balefire: A fire lit for magical purposes, usually outdoors.

Casting a circle: The process of drawing a circle around oneself to seal out unfriendly influences and raise magical power. It is the first step in a spell.

Censer: An incense burner. Traditionally a censer is a metal container, filled with incense, that is swung on the end of a chain.

Censing: The process of burning incense to spiritually cleanse an object.

Centering yourself: To prepare for a magical rite by calming and centering all of your personal energy.

Chakra: One of the seven centers of spiritual energy in the human body, according to the philosophy of yoga.

Charging: To infuse an object with magical power.

Circle of protection: A circle cast to protect oneself from unfriendly influences.

Crystals: Quartz or other stones that store cleansing or protective energies.

Deosil: Clockwise movement, symbolic of life and positive energies.

Deva: A divine being according to Hindu beliefs; a devil or evil spirit according to Zoroastrianism.

Direct/retrograde: Refers to the motion of a planet when seen from the earth. A planet is "direct" when it appears to be moving forward from the point of view of a person on the earth. It is "retrograde" when it appears to be moving backward.

Dowsing: To use a divining rod to search for a thing, usually water or minerals.

Dowsing pendulum: A long cord with a coin or gem at one end. The pattern of its swing is used to answer questions.

Dryad: A tree spirit or forest guardian.

Fey: An archaic term for a magical spirit or a fairylike being.

Gris-gris: A small bag containing charms, herbs, stones, and other items to draw energy, luck, love, or prosperity to the wearer.

Mantra: A sacred chant used in Hindu tradition to embody the divinity invoked; it is said to possess deep magical power.

Needfire: A ceremonial fire kindled at dawn on major Wiccan holidays. It was traditionally used to light all other household fires.

Pentagram: A symbolically protective five-pointed star with one point upward.

Power hand: The dominant hand; the hand used most often.

Scry: To predict the future by gazing at or into an object such as a crystal ball or pool of water.

Second sight: The psychic power or ability to foresee the future.

Sigil: A personal seal or symbol.

Smudge/smudge stick: To spiritually cleanse an object by waving smoke over and around it. A smudge stick is a bundle of several incense sticks.

Wand: A stick or rod used for casting circles and as a focus for magical power.

Widdershins: Counterclockwise movement, symbolic of negative magical purposes, sometimes used to disperse negative energies.

Spell Notes

Spell Notes

Llewellyn's 2017 Witches' Calendar

Captivating original artwork and a rich array of content have made *Llewellyn's Witches' Calendar*—now in its eighteenth year—the top-selling calendar of its kind. Enjoy new, enchanting scratchboard illustrations by award-winning artist Kathleen Edwards. Each month also offers an inspiring article, plus a spell or ritual. Discover love potions and poppets in February, sip the season's spirits in October, and make a solstice wish in December. Astrological data and magical correspondences are also included.

978-0-7387-3765-2, 28 pp., 12 x 12 $13.99

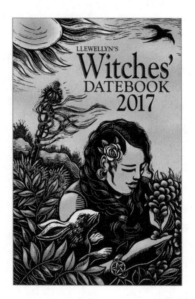

Llewellyn's 2017 Witches' Datebook

Keep up with the increasing busyness of life—both magical and mundane—with *Llewellyn's Witches' Datebook*, now featuring enchanting illustrations from award-winning artist Kathleen Edwards. Add a little magic to each day and keep pace with the ever-turning Wheel of the Year with this indispensable, on-the-go tool.

Find fresh ways to celebrate the sacred seasons and enhance your practice with Anglo-Saxon traditions (Alaric Albertsson), inspiring Sabbat musings (Thuri Calafia), tasty Sabbat recipes (Monica Crosson), and magical gemstones (Ember Grant). Astrological information and daily colors are included for spellwork.

978-0-7387-767-6, 144 pp., 5¼ x 8 $11.99

To order, call 1-877-NEW-WRLD
Prices subject to change without notice
Order at Llewellyn.com 24 hours a day, 7 days a week!

Llewellyn's 2017

Sabbats

ALMANAC

Samhain 2016
to
Mabon 2017

Rituals • Crafts • Recipes • Folklore